Pg 133

The Meal That Heals

The Meal That Heals

The Completely Updated and Expanded Version

By Perry Stone, Jr.

ISBN: 0-9708611-8-4

LOC: 2006903381

Copyright 2006 by Voice of Evangelism, Inc.

Voice of Evangelism Outreach Ministries, Inc.
P. O. Box 3595
Cleveland, Tennessee, 37320
TEL: 423 – 478-3456
FAX: 423-478-1392
Internet: perrystone.org

Printed in the United States of America
Pathway Press, 1080 Montgomery Avenue,
Cleveland, Tennessee 37311

Contents

Dedication

I am grateful for the eye-opening research of Dr. John Miller, whose spiritual insight into this subject opened my eyes to a fresh truth that had been hidden by centuries of tradition.

This book is a combination of my personal notes over many years of ministry, plus insight from Dr. Miller during our Manna-Fest television programs called *The Meal that Heals.*

I pray this truth will become a life-changing revelation to you; and that for the remaining days of your life, you will view Communion in a new and exciting way and receive the benefits Christ intended for your body, soul and spirit!

I dedicate this new edition of *The Meal that Heals* to Dr. Miller, and appreciate his willingness to allow us to get this message out to as many people as possible.

Introduction

Years ago I became acquainted with "Doc" Miller, a special man licensed in four areas of the healing arts. One afternoon after service, we began to fellowship around the Word of God. Dr. Miller began explaining a "revelation" from the Scripture to me that I had never heard. He expounded the concept of receiving daily Communion as a way of receiving your healing.

A fourth generation minister who was raised in a Christian church, I was very familiar with the Lord's Supper (Communion). I had been taught that the Lord's Supper was administered only by an ordained minister, once a month or perhaps several times a year, in local congregations. I was uncertain that the concept of receiving Communion every day at home was a sound Biblical idea.

I set out to research the idea of receiving Communion at home for intimate fellowship with the Lord and for healing. The more I researched and the more I heard Dr. Miller's explanations, the more I became convinced that it was not only Biblical, but that daily Communion from house to house was practiced by first century Christians. As a Roman-style church system developed throughout the Mediterranean area, it seems that man-made traditions eventually stopped this practice.

For several years we have aired special interviews with Dr. Miller on television as he expounded on the teaching of receiving daily Communion for healing. These powerful instructional series were aired on our program, *Manna-Fest*. We recorded the programs on two DVDs for home viewing and printed a 70-page book, giving more instruction on this subject.

Since that time, substantial research and fresh illumination on the subject has led to this new edition of *The Meal That Heals*. You may have read the first edition of this book, but I have completely re-written it, giving you fresh insight and deeper explanations to add to your spiritual knowledge and understanding. This additional teaching will also increase your faith to believe God for your own healing.

We know that if Christ tarries, we will eventually pass on and depart this life (Hebrews 9:27). We must determine to not depart this life before our appointed time, however; and we must endeavor to fulfill all that God has for us in this life (Ecclesiastes 7:17).

It is important for you to understand your healing covenant with God because sickness and disease are so prevalent in the earth. We must fight the good fight of faith with spiritual weapons, and one of those *covenant* weapons is Communion.

I believe it is God's will to satisfy us with long life and to show us His salvation (Psalms 91:16). As you study this book, soak in the revelation of the Word and allow the Holy Spirit to speak to you. Then in faith, put into action what you learn.

God bless and keep you is my prayer!

Preaching the Power of the Covenant

Perry Stone, Jr.

God's Covenant Of Healing for His Children

Bless the Lord, O my soul, and forget not all
His benefits: who forgives all your iniquities,
who heals all your diseases *(Psalm 103:2, 3).*

What comes to your mind when I say, "You are saved?" To most Christians, salvation means the gift of eternal life through receiving Christ and repenting of sins (Ephesians 2:5). Salvation is the key to entering heaven.

In the New Testament, however, the word *saved* has a much broader meaning. The Greek word for *saved* is used

57 times in the English translation of the Bible; and in all but five references, it is the same Greek word, *sozo*, which means "to save, deliver, protect, and heal" (*Strong's Concordance*). Thus, salvation is a complete work of making a person whole in spirit, soul and body.

In the ministry of Christ, the Bible declared that those He healed were "made whole." The woman with the issue of blood touched His garment to be made whole (Matthew 9:21). When her faith touched Christ and she was healed, Christ said, "Thy faith hath made thee whole" (Matthew 9:22).

Then we read, "The woman was made whole from that hour" (Matthew 9:22). Three times in this narrative, the word "whole" is used. This Greek word is *sozo*, the exact same word translated 52 times as the word "saved."

The point is that most Christian churches identify being saved only as having your sins forgiven. God's Word, however, makes no theological distinction between sickness of the spirit and sickness of the body, as the traditional church does. God's will is to "forgive all your iniquities and heal all your diseases" (Psalms 103:3).

God's will is for believers to be made whole and to walk in wholeness and blessing during their lifetimes.

The most common Greek word translated "whole" in 1 Thessalonians 5:23 is *holos,* which means "altogether." When the body, soul and spirit are functioning in harmony as one healthy, strong unit, then a person is whole.

God's Healing Covenant

The first Biblical reference to healing was when Abraham, God's covenant man, prayed for King Abimelech and his wife to have children. Although she was barren, she later bore children (Genesis 20:17).

The next reference to God's healing power is in Exodus 15:26, where God makes a healing covenant with the entire Hebrew nation after they came out of Egypt:

> And said, If you will diligently heed the voice of the Lord your God and do what is right in His sight, give ear to His commandments and keep all His statutes, I will put none of the diseases on you which I have brought on the Egyptians. For I am the Lord who heals you (*Exodus 15:26*).

God announced that He was the "Lord who heals you." Throughout the Old Testament there are about 16 compound names for God; that is, a Hebrew name combining two Hebraic words which reveal a particular nature or character of God. Among the Hebrew names are:

Hebrew Name	English Meaning	Reference
Jehovah-Jireh	God will provide	Genesis 22:14
Jehovah-Shalom	God our peace	Judges 6:24
Jehovah-Tsidkeenu	God our righteousness	Jeremiah 23:6
Jehovah-Sabaoth	God of hosts	1 Samuel 1:3
Jehovah-Shammah	God is present	Ezekiel 48:35
Jehovah-Elyon	God most high	Psalm 7:17

In Exodus 15:26, God introduced Himself as healer through a new name, *Jehovah Raphah!* The Hebrew word *rapha* is a word alluding to "stitching something that has been torn." It means to completely repair something that needs mending. Figuratively, it means to cure someone.

This is more than just another name for God. In Exodus 15:26, God made a *healing covenant* for His people as they came out of Egypt. Numerous diseases and sickness in Egypt could spread like a plague throughout the population. God knew the Hebrews needed protection from these diseases. *K K.*

God's covenant of healing stated, "If you will obey My Word and walk in My commandments, I will prevent disease from coming on you." When Israel came out of bondage, the Bible says, "[God] brought them forth also with silver and gold, and there was not one feeble person among their tribes" (Psalm 105:37).

Imagine over 600,000 men, not counting the women and children, who marched through the Red Sea, healed and ready for their journey. God keeps His promises! Weeks later, the Hebrews began to break the commandments of God by worshiping a golden calf.

Imagine over 600,000 marching through the Red Sea, healed and ready for the journey.

In the wilderness, they forgot their promise and sinned against God. Bitterly, they complained against God's plan for their deliverance. As a result, fiery serpents and plagues were sent among the people (Numbers 21).

The cause was the people, not God. His people broke the covenant and, as a result, suffered from their acts of disobedience. Throughout the Old Testament, we see many other examples of God's healing power being manifested through prayer and faith in God's Word:

✝ Miriam was healed of leprosy through Moses' prayers (*Numbers 12:13-15*).

✝ Naaman the Syrian was healed as he dipped in the Jordan River (*2 Kings 5*).

✝ King Hezekiah was healed as he prayed to God (*2 Kings 20*).

The final Book of the Old Testament, Malachi, prophesies about the healing power of God which would arise through the "Sun of righteousness," the future Messiah.

But to you who fear My name the Sun of Righteousness shall arise with healing in His wings; and you shall go out and grow fat like stall-fed calves (*Malachi 4:2*).

The Messiah brings spiritual light into the world in the same manner that the sun illuminates the earth. The phrase "healing in His wings" alludes to the Messiah bringing healing to the nations.

The Hebrew word "wings" is *kanaph*, and can allude to the edge of a garment. In Jewish belief, this is the imagery of the prayer shawl that Jewish men wore which had fringes (large threads) draping from the bottom.

This shawl is still worn when attending the synagogue or prayer gatherings, or for special religious occasions.

Christ wore this type of garment, and it was the "hem of the garment" (the threads) that the woman with the issue of blood touched when she was made whole (Matthew 9:20-22).

By faith, she pulled on the string of Jesus' garment; and she actually pulled healing virtue (power) out of Christ's body into her body. She felt the healing occur instantly. This was a fulfillment of what Malachi saw.

The Healing Covenant in the New Testament

This covenant of healing continued through the entire ministry of Christ. The four Gospels reveal four main levels of healing manifested through Christ's ministry:

1. Miracles of physical healing (*Matthew 8:16*)

2. Miracles of casting out spirits (*Mark 1:34*)

3. Creative miracles (*Luke 22:51*)

4. Special miracles (*John 2:3-10*)

Christ's miracles included healing the sick and diseased, and opening the eyes of the blind and the ears of the deaf. He caused the dumb (the mute who were unable to talk) to speak again. His delivering ministry included healing the lepers, raising the dead and a host of other miracles not recorded in the Scripture (John 21:25).

Creative miracles were not unusual. They included the multiplying of bread and fish, among other things. A special miracle restored a man's ear that had been severed from his head (Luke 22:51). Another miracle turned the water into wine (John 2:3-10).

He commissioned His disciples to go forth preaching the Kingdom of God and healing the sick in every city where they ministered.

Not only did Christ perform miracles, but He commissioned His disciples to go forth preaching the Kingdom of God and healing the sick in every city where they ministered:

> Then He called His twelve disciples together and gave them power and authority over all demons, and to cure diseases. He sent them to preach the kingdom of God and to heal the sick (*Luke 9:1, 2*).

Christ also appointed 70 men to go out in teams of two. They were to preach, to heal the sick and to cast out evil spirits. Luke records the spiritual success these men had in their ministry:

> Then the seventy returned with joy, saying, "Lord, even the demons are subject to us in Your name" (*Luke 10:17*).

Some ministers teach that a healing anointing was given only to the original 12 apostles, to assist in the birth of the Christian church. The healing anointing was not confined to them, however. Throughout the Book of Acts, men who were not apostles ministered healing to the sick.

Such was the case when a deacon named Ananias laid his hands on Saul of Tarsus who was instantly healed of blindness (Acts 9:12-18).

Although not one of the original 12 apostles, Philip prayed and saw miracles of healing and people delivered from evil spirits as he ministered in Samaria (Acts 8).

James wrote that the *elders* of the church could anoint the sick with oil and pray the prayer of faith over them, and God would heal the afflicted person (James 5:16). Only religious theological tradition limits God's healing covenant to a certain period of history.

Healing in Church History

The theory that gifts of healing ceased after the death of the last apostle (John) is widely taught in churches throughout North America. This idea is the tradition of liberal theologians and is not in agreement with actual church history.

The early church fathers wrote of the continuation of miracles among believers in the church.

> For numberless demoniacs throughout the whole world, and in your city, many of our Christian men exorcising them in the name of Jesus Christ, who was crucified under Pontius Pilate, have healed and do heal, rendering helpless and driving the possessing devils out of the men, though they could not be cured by all the other exorcists, and those who used incantations and drugs (Justin Martyr, *Apologetics II, Chapter 6. A.D. 165.*)

> Those who are in truth His disciples, receiving grace from Him, do in His name perform [miracles]. . . . For some do certainly and truly drive out devils, so that those who have thus been cleansed from evil spirits frequently both believe [in Christ], and join themselves to the

Church. Others still, heal the sick by laying their hands upon them, and they are made whole. Yea, moreover, as I have said, the dead even have been raised up, and remained among us for many years (Irenaeus, *Adversus Haereses.* Book II, 32:4. A.D. 200).

And some give evidence of their having received through this faith a marvelous power by the cures which they perform, invoking no other name over those who need their help than that of the God of all things, and of Jesus, along with a mention of His history. For by these means we too have seen many persons freed from grievous calamities, and from distractions of mind, and madness, and countless other ills, which could be cured neither by men nor devils (Origen, *Contra Celsum. Book III, Chapter 24.* A.D. 250).

Clement mentioned, in A.D. 275, "men who have received the gift of healing with confidence, to the glory of God" (*Epistle to the Corinthians*). In 429, Theodor of Mopsueste said, "Many heathen amongst us are being healed by Christians from whatsoever sickness they have, so abundant are the miracles in our midst" (Theodor Christlieb, *Modern Doubt and Christian Belief,* page 321).

Healings and miracles began with Abraham and continued through the New Testament and into the first centuries of the church, because healing is a part of God's nature and a part of God's Word.

One man said, "We no longer need miracles because we have the Bible." I suggest we can have miracles because the Bible says we can, and because healing is a part of our covenant with God!

Healing Is a Covenant

In the Bible we find that there is no such thing as a "day of miracles," or a "day of healing." There is only a covenant of healing that has been established by God. This covenant of healing can be seen through the several different methods of healing found in the Bible.

According to Dr. John Miller, the four Gospels record the stories of 19 people delivered through the ministry of Jesus. The problems of 11 of them were caused by spirits (Luke 4:33, Luke 9:42, Luke 13:11); others received healing from diseases that affected their bodies. Miracles operate through at least four avenues:

> 1. Miracles that happen through signs and wonders (*Hebrews 2:4*)

2. Miracles that happen because of an anointing (*Acts 10:38*)

3. Miracles that happen through a deliverance (*Luke 4:18*)

4. Miracles that happen through faith in the atonement (*1 Peter 2:24*)

In the Bible, there are six covenant methods for healing. While many scriptures back up each method, I will talk only about the last one. Healing can come through:

✝ The laying on of hands (*Mark16:18*)

✝ Anointing with oil and praying in faith (*James 5:14, 15*)

✝ Gifts of healing and miracles (*1 Corinthians 12:7-10*)

✝ The spoken Word (*Psalm 107:20*)

✝ An act of obedience (*John 9:6, 7*)

✝ Receiving Communion (*1 Corinthians 11:25-31*)

Of these examples, we will examine the importance of receiving Communion for intimacy with Christ and for daily healing. This method, I believe, has not been emphasized as much as the others; yet it may be the most important way to walk in wholeness of body, soul and spirit.

2/19

Understanding the Act of Communion

> The cup of blessing which we bless, is it not the communion of the blood of Christ? The bread which we break, is it not the communion of the body of Christ (*1 Corinthians 10:16*).

What does it mean when we speak of *receiving Communion*? Christians from most churches identify this as a sacred time set aside by the leadership of the congregation for believers to come together and receive the bread and the fruit of the vine. These elements are received as reminders of Christ's finished work on the Cross, and to celebrate the promise of Christ's return.

For many believers this special gathering, called by most ministers "the Communion" or "Lord's Supper," is celebrated once a week, once a month or once a year. Ministers call the bread and the fruit (or juice) of the vine "the Sacrament."

A classical Latin word *sacrament,* referred to the oath of faithfulness a soldier took to his commander. Religiously, it is from Pliny's letter to Trajan (c. 112), telling of Christians who bound themselves with a sacrament or "oath" (*sacramento*) to be faithful to Christ and abstain from crimes (Pliny, *Letters* 10.96, 97. Tr. William Whiston).

Protestants observe two sacraments, baptism and Communion; while Catholics and the Greek Orthodox add to this list, "confirmation, penance, extreme unction, ordination and matrimony."

Catholics participate in what is called the *Mass.* In this rite, the priest offers the bread and the wine, called the *Eucharist.* The word comes from ancient Greek and means *to give thanks* or *thanksgiving.* The Greek word is found in Matthew 15:36, 16:27, Mark 8:6; 14:23, and other places.

Today, we give thanks by "saying grace" at the dinner table. Thus the Eucharist is the blessing of the elements of communion.

Two Views of Communion

Catholics believe that in the Eucharist the bread becomes the literal body of Christ and the wine becomes the literal blood of Christ. This teaching is called *transubstantiation*. They say that in the Mass, the same sacrifice Jesus offered on the Cross is offered again. This doctrine states that somehow the bread and fruit of the vine are miraculously converted into the literal body and blood of Jesus when blessed by the priest before it is administered.

> Transubstantiation is . . . the belief that at the "moment" of Consecration [by a priest or church official], the elements . . . of bread and wine are . . . not only spiritually transformed, but are actually (substantially) transformed into the Body and Blood of Christ. The elements retain the appearance . . . of bread and wine, but are indeed the actual Body and Blood of Christ, the true, real, and substantial presence of Jesus in the Eucharist (*The Catholic Encyclopedia, Volume V* on CD-Rom, © 1909).

This view says that while the bread still looks, feels, smells and tastes like bread, it literally becomes the flesh of Jesus. Thus, everyone who eats the bread of Communion eats Jesus' flesh, whether he eats in faith or in unbelief.

The problem with this view is it places Jesus' body and blood here on earth every time someone celebrates the Lord's Supper.

> *Jesus is now in heaven, at the right hand of the Father (Acts 7:55, Ephesians 1:20).*

This cannot be the case. The Scripture says that Jesus is right now in heaven, at the right hand of the Father (Acts 7:55, Ephesians 1:20, Colossians 3:1, Hebrews 8:1, 1 Peter 3:22).

On the other hand, most Lutherans believe in a doctrine called *consubstantiation*. This means that in Communion, the body and blood of Christ, and the bread and wine, *coexist* in union with each other. They believe that the fundamental substance of the body and blood of Christ are present alongside the bread and cup.

This confusion comes from misunderstanding the words of Jesus in John 6:53: "Most assuredly, I say to you, unless you eat the flesh of the Son of Man and drink His blood, you have no life in you."

Consubstantiation is the view that the bread and cup of Communion coexist and are equal to the flesh and blood of Jesus, but still remain bread and wine. *Transubstantiation* is the view that the bread and the wine become the actual body and blood of Jesus.

The correct view is a third view.

After Jesus took the bread and the fruit of the vine, He gave these elements to the disciples and said, "This is My body . . . this is My blood" (Matthew 26:26-28). He was not speaking literally because He still possessed His literal body and blood! At the same time, Christ specifically identified the drink as "this fruit of the vine" in verse 29. The physical nature of the elements had not changed.

Christ was representing His body and blood by comparing them to the bread and the fruit of the vine of Communion. Jesus often spoke in metaphors, a figure of speech which represents *that very thing*. Jesus referred to Herod as a fox in Luke 13:32, but He was not saying the ruler had become a four-legged animal. Jesus said, "I am the vine, you are the branches," in John 15:5; but He did not mean He had become a piece of vegetation.

Jesus said of the rite of Communion, "Do this in re-membrance of Me" in Luke 22:19, implying that although He would not be physically present, the covenant He was establishing would continue to be in effect as they participated in Communion. We are to have continuity with the practice of Jesus. The Bible says:

> And as they were eating, Jesus took bread, blessed and broke it, and gave it to the disciples and said, "Take, eat; this is My body." Then He took the cup, and gave thanks, and gave it to them, saying, "Drink from it, all of you. For this is My blood of the new covenant, which is shed for many for the remission of sins" (*Matthew 25:26-28*).

If Jesus was turning the bread into His literal body, then He was in His body while holding another body in His hand. Although He was God and man, He did not have two physical bodies.

Another point is that if Jesus' literal body and blood are already here on earth every time we partake of Communion, then why does He need to come again? He is already here in many bodies if either transubstantiation or consubstantiation is a fact!

In the 19th century, Bishop J. C. Ryle wrote in *Light from Old Times*, that if you believe the bread and cup become the actual body and blood of Christ in the partaking of Communion, you are denying three things:

1. You are denying Christ's finished work on the Cross. Jesus cried, "It is finished" A sacrifice that needs to be repeated is neither a perfect nor a complete sacrifice.

2. You are denying the priestly office of Christ. If the Communion elements were His literal body and blood, then the elements themselves would become the sacrifice for sin. For anyone besides Christ to offer our Lord's body and blood to God as a sacrifice for sin is to rob our great High Priest of His glory.

If anyone besides Christ can offer our Lord's body as a sacrifice for sin, then our High Priest is robbed of His glory.

3. You are denying Christ's human nature. If His literal body can be in more than one place at the same time, then He did not have a body like ours, and Jesus was not the "last Adam" in that He did not have our nature (*Light from Old Times*, pp. 58, 59).

The bread and wine *represent* the body and blood of Jesus. They do not in any way become the literal body and blood themselves. We do not literally chew on Jesus' flesh with our teeth or drink His literal blood with our mouths.

But by eating this bread in faith, we have *communion* with the real, physical body of Christ. By drinking this wine in faith, we have *communion* with the real, physical blood of Christ.

Among both Protestant and Catholic groups, importance is placed on the bread and the wine, or juice. The main difference is Protestants believe the bread and wine *represent* the body and blood of Christ and the Catholics believe the bread and wine *become* the literal body and blood of Christ.

In Scripture, the word *Communion* is used four times: 1 Corinthians 10:16; 2 Corinthians 6:14; 13:14. Twice, it alludes to the Lord's Supper. "Communion" comes from a Greek word *koinonia*, which means intimate partnership or intercourse. It is a very personal and intimate word.

How Did Communion Come About?

Over 3,500 years ago the Hebrew people had become slaves to the Egyptians. The king of Egypt, or Pharaoh, was unwilling to release the Hebrews and allow them to return to Israel. God sent 10 plagues on Egypt.

The end result was that the Pharaoh released the Hebrew nation, consisting of 600,000 men of war, not counting the women and children (Exodus 12:37). The 10th plague involved the death angel moving from house to house and taking the lives of the firstborn, both men and beasts (Exodus 11:5).

To protect the Hebrews from the destroying angel, God required each Hebrew family to take a young lamb, place the blood on the left, right and top posts of the door to the house, and eat all of the lamb before midnight (Exodus 12:7, 8).

The miracle was two-fold: they were healed and they were protected. By eating the lamb, the Hebrews experienced supernatural healing, as indicated in Psalm 105:37:

He brought them forth also with silver and gold: and there was not one feeble person among their tribes.

The other miracle was that the blood on the outside doorposts restrained the destroying angel from entering the homes marked with lamb's blood. Thus the Hebrew family was protected from both sickness and death as a result of the blood and body of the lamb.

"When I see the blood, I will pass over you, and the plague shall not be upon you. . . ."

God promised that their obedience of marking the door by the lamb's blood would cause death to "pass over" their houses:

And the blood shall be to you for a token upon the houses where ye are: and when I see the blood, I will pass over you, and the plague shall not be upon you to destroy you, when I smite the land of Egypt *(Exodus 12:13)*.

God told the Hebrews that this event would be a memorial forever. On the 14th day of Nisan, the entire nation of Israel was to celebrate a Passover, reminding the proceeding generations of how God brought Israel out of Egypt with mighty signs and wonders (Leviticus 23:5).

The Hebrew word for "Passover" is *Pesach*, and alludes to "skipping over, to leap or to dance." The word indicates how God required the angel of death to skip over the homes of the Hebrews that were protected by the lamb's blood.

Each year religious Jews conduct a Passover *seder* in which they tell the amazing story of the deliverance from Egypt. During this season bread is baked without leaven, recalling how the Hebrews did not have time to put leaven in their bread before departing from Egypt.

Also, four different cups of wine are used, each cup identifying a different aspect of the Passover story. These cups are numbered and named:

✚ The first cup is called the cup of **sanctification.**

✚ The second cup is called the cup of **affliction.**

✚ The third cup is the cup of **redemption.**

✚ The fourth cup is the cup of **consummation** or **Hallel.**

The Lord's Supper

Prior to His trial and crucifixion, Christ met in a large room with His disciples. That evening Christ made an announcement. Most scholars believe that as Christ held up the third cup, the cup of redemption, He amazed His disciples by His actions:

> Likewise also the cup after supper, saying, this cup is the New Testament in my blood, which is shed for you *(Luke 22:20)*.

Christ was introducing a new covenant that would be sealed with His own blood. No longer would future Hebrew believers emphasize their deliverance from Egypt. Instead, each time they took the cup and bread, they would celebrate a spiritual freedom, a deliverance from death and hell, and the promise of eternal life!

It would be this act, known as Communion, which would be the central ordinance among all future Christians around the world!

The Prophetic Fulfillment of Passover

Christ's crucifixion was the perfect prophetic fulfillment of the ancient Passover in Egypt. Pharaoh was a picture of Satan who held us in bondage, and Egypt was a type of the world system.

The blood of the lamb in Egypt was a type and shadow of the precious blood of Jesus, identified as the "Lamb of God" (John 1:29). Three marks of blood were to be made on the door of the Hebrew homes in Egypt. They were to be located on the left, right and top posts (Exodus 12:7).

The amazing correlation is there were three crosses, hanging with victims on them, at the time of Christ's crucifixion. A thief hung on the left side and one hung on the right. Christ was in the middle (Matthew 27:38).

Another fantastic parallel between the ancient patterns of redemption and the crucifixion is identified in the Day of Atonement ritual, called *Yom ha Kippur*. On this sixth feast of Israel, the High priest brought two identical goats before him. He marked one for the Lord and the other for Azazel (Leviticus 16).

The Lord's goat was slaughtered and burned on the Temple altar. The priest laid hands on the head of the "Azazel" goat, transferring the sins of Israel to this particular goat. Called the *scapegoat*, it was led into the wilderness by a priest with a rope. There, it was eventually pushed off a rugged mountain ledge to its death.

Another Day of Atonement tradition developed with three red, 18-inch threads. The priest tied one to the goat for the Lord, and another to the head of the scapegoat.

The third thread was hung from the door of the Temple in Jerusalem. Jewish tradition says that when the scapegoat died in the wilderness, the red thread on the Temple door turned white, indicating that Israel's sins were remitted and forgiven!

This is why Isaiah wrote, "Though your sins are like scarlet, they shall be as white as snow; though they are red like crimson, they shall be as wool" (Isaiah 1:18). These three red threads correlate with the three men hanging on the three crosses on Golgotha. One Man, Christ, was dying "for the Lord." Another man, a bitter thief, died in his sin (like the scapegoat).

The third man, another thief, changed his eternal destiny while hanging beside Jesus. His sins became "as white as snow" in the same manner of the red thread turning white on the Temple doors, indicating remission of sins!

The Crucifixion story shows a correlation between Christ's death and the two identical goats. One goat died at the Temple; the other was released in the wilderness to die later. Christ was the sacrifice dying in Jerusalem. In mock symbolism, Pilate transferred responsibility for the sins commited that day to the people; who, in turn, chose Barabbas. He was released by Pilate prior to the crucifixion (Matthew 27:16).

Both Passover and the Day of Atonement are prophetic pictures of the redemption of mankind. . . .

The name *Barabbas* is interesting. *Bar* means "son," and *Abbas* means "exalted father." Jesus was the son of the Father, and Barabbas had an "exalted" earthly father.

The name of Jesus in Hebrew is *Yeshuah*, and one tradition says it was the actual first name of Barabbas. This indicates that both Christ and Barabbas had the same first names, just as both goats on the Day of Atonement were identical. The difference is that Jesus died as Lord, and Barabbas escaped as a sinner, dying later in his sins.

Both Passover and the Day of Atonement prophetically depict the redemption of mankind through the suffering and resurrection of Christ! Jewish and Messianic believers celebrate Passover each spring as a reminder of God's mighty deliverance in bringing His people out of Egypt.

Back to the Communion Supper

In the Christian church, believers recognize the historical application of Passover, and see its prophetic fulfillment in Christ who, as God's final lamb, died during Passover (Matthew 26:19).

Just as the Jewish Passover reminds Hebrews of their great day of redemption from Egypt and their future promise of inheriting the Promised Land, so Christian Communion is a reminder of our redemption through Christ's suffering, and of our future inheritance with Christ in heaven!

During the first Passover, the flesh of a lamb was eaten at the table of Hebrew families, and the lamb's flesh brought supernatural healing for the journey through the wilderness. The blood on the door stopped the destroying angel from taking the life of the firstborn. Thus, the body and the blood of the Passover lamb brought complete healing and redemption.

The body of Christ, God's final lamb, brought healing through the wounds and stripes on His body, as well as salvation through His blood on the cross. Communion is a sign of our belief in Christ's finished work and a testimony of our faith in the completed work of salvation.

How often should a believer receive Communion? How often did the first century believers receive Communion? Part of the answer lies with understanding the term, "breaking of bread."

What It Means to
Break Bread

And they, continuing daily with one accord
in the temple, and breaking bread from
house to house, did eat their meat with
gladness and singleness of heart (*Acts 2:46*).

This book deals with receiving Communion daily,
especially for your healing. Is there Biblical prece-
dent of early believers receiving Communion every day?
Or was it just during certain marked occasions?

To understand the concept of receiving Communion every day, one must examine the Book of Acts and the existing historical records of first century Christians. Two passages in the New Testament indicate that believers went from house to house *breaking bread*. What is the original meaning of this phrase and how does it relate to daily Communion?

The Breaking of Bread

There are also two main references in the New Testament where we are told that Jesus broke bread:

> And as they were eating, Jesus took bread, and blessed and broke it, and gave it to the disciples and said, "Take, eat; this is My body" (*Matthew 26:26*).

At this event, the Last Supper, Christ introduced the New Covenant to His disciples. After the Resurrection, Christ met with His disciples to again break bread:

> Now it came to pass, as He sat at the table with them, that He took bread, blessed and broke it, and gave it to them (*Luke 24:30*).

At the Last Supper with Jesus and the disciples, the cup of consummation (the fourth cup) is mentioned (Matthew

26:29). The fourth cup of wine, however, is not mentioned *after* the Resurrection account, only that Christ broke bread with them (Luke 24). This is because Christ had already stated that He would not drink from the fourth cup again until He drank it anew in the Kingdom:

> But I say to you, I will not drink of this fruit of the vine from now on until that day when I drink it new with you in My Father's kingdom (*Matthew 26:29*).

This glorious promise of "drinking the cup in the Kingdom" alludes to the future Marriage Supper of the Lamb, where the saints who have received the New Covenant of Christ's blood will seal and consummate their marriage to the glorious Lamb of God at a wedding supper in heaven (Revelation 19:9).

"Drinking the cup in the Kingdom" alludes to the future Marriage Supper of the Lamb. . .

Shortly after Christ's resurrection, He appeared to two men on the road to Emmaus. They were unaware that it was Christ as He expounded the prophecies concerning the Messiah to them.

Christ was invited into their house, and there He "broke bread with them." Suddenly, "Their eyes were opened and they knew him" (Luke 24:31). Then we read:

> And they told about the things that had happened on the road, and how He was known to them in the breaking of bread (*Luke 24:35*).

This event initiated a continual custom or tradition among the first century believers; breaking bread from house to house and celebrating the resurrection of Christ and the promise that He would return again for them. This breaking of bread was a term used in the Bible to describe the fellowship of the Lord's Table, or the Communion being practiced in the homes of believers.

The House-to-House References

The first converts to Christ were people who were Hebrews. The church was birthed on the Hebrew Feast of Pentecost, and over 3,000 Jewish converts were baptized in water (Acts 2:1-20).

Shortly after this, persecution broke out in Jerusalem. Eventually it became risky for Hebrew believers to worship at the Temple (Acts 4; Acts 5:20-40; Acts 21:27-31).

Paul confessed to persecuting believers from city to city before his conversion (Acts 26:11). This persecution led believers to worship in the homes of fellow believers (Acts 5:42). Eventually, churches were begun in believers' houses. This was the safest place to meet and worship in smaller groups without the threat of religious leaders from the synagogues or persecution from certain Pharisees, Sadducees and Temple priests.

In home groups, believers would study, pray and sing hymns (Ephesians 5:19). The Bible reveals the names of several believers whose homes became churches:

> Aquilla and Priscilla had a church in their house (*Romans 16:5*).
>
> Nymphas at Laodicea had a church in his house (*Colossians 4:15*).
>
> Apphia and Archippus had a church in their house (*Philemon 1:2*).

It also appears that believers met, at times, on the "first day of the week" (Acts 20:7; 1 Corinthians 16:2). During these times they would "break bread." The first day of the week on the Jewish calendar would be Sunday.

> On the first day of the week, when the disciples came together to break bread, Paul, ready to depart the next day, spoke to them and

continued his message until midnight (*Acts 20:7*).

The Scriptures indicate the practice of breaking bread was a central part of the early activity among believers in their homes.

> So continuing daily with one accord in the temple, and breaking bread from house to house, they ate their food with gladness and simplicity of heart (*Acts 2:46*).

> And day after day they regularly assembled in the temple with united purpose, and in their homes they broke bread [including the Lord's Supper]. They partook of their food with gladness and simplicity and generous hearts (*Acts 2:46*, AMP).

When I was growing up in church, the Sunday evening services were thought to be more exciting and "spiritual" than the Sunday morning services. The Sunday evenings were called "camp meeting" services.

After the services were over, it was common for the believers to go out and fellowship at a local restaurant (usually fast food or pizza). This is where we spent time talking about the Word, and getting to know each other. We called it "breaking bread."

For years when I read where the early church broke bread from house to house, I assumed it alluded to simply having a dinner in someone's house. Only recently did I research the true meaning of this term. I discovered the real reason it was an important daily activity to those early saints.

According to numerous Christian commentaries that I have studied, the daily breaking of bread was serving the Lord's Supper (Communion) in believers' homes!

Remember, the original Passover supper was served in Hebrew homes in Egypt, and the Lord's Supper was initially instituted for us by Christ in a home!

Just as the original Passover originated in the home, so the Lord's Supper was instituted by Christ in a home!

Here are the comments from nine different commentaries on "breaking of bread from house to house." Scripture references: Acts 2:42, Acts 20:7, 1 Corinthians 10:16.

Breaking of bread. The Syriac renders this "the eucharist" or the Lord's Supper (*Barnes Notes on the New Testament*).

And in breaking of bread. Whether this means the holy eucharist, or their common meals, it is difficult to say. The Syriac understands it of the former. Breaking of bread was that act which preceded a feast or meal, and which was performed by the master of the house, when he pronounced the blessing-what we would call grace before meat (*Adam Clarke's Commentary on the Bible*).

And in breaking of bread. From Acts 20:7,11, and 1 Corinthians 10:16, it seems pretty certain that partaking of the Lord's Supper is what is here meant. But just as when the Lord's Supper was first instituted it was preceded by the full paschal meal, so a frugal repast seems for a considerable time to have preceded the Eucharistic feast (Jamieson, Fausset, and Brown, *Critical Commentary on the Whole Bible*).

They frequently joined in the ordinance of the Lord's supper. They continued in **the breaking of bread**, in celebrating that memorial of their Master's death, as those that were not ashamed to own their relation to, and their dependence upon, Christ and him crucified. They could not forget the death of Christ, yet they kept up this memorial of it, and made it their constant practice, because it was an institution of Christ.

They **broke bread from house to house**; kat' oikon—house by house; they did not think fit to celebrate the eucharist in the Temple, for that was peculiar to the Christian institutes, and therefore they administered that ordinance in private houses, choosing such houses of the converted Christians as were convenient, to which the neighbors resorted; and they went from one to another of these little synagogues or domestic chapels, houses that had churches in them, and there celebrated the eucharist with those that usually met there to worship God (*Matthew Henry's Commentary*).

It is generally supposed that the early disciples attached so much significance to **the breaking of bread** at the ordinary meals, more than our saying grace, that they followed the meal with the Lord's Supper. Hence what is referred to here is the Lord's Supper following the ordinary meal (Robertson's *Word Pictures of the New Testament*).

The breaking of bread, the administering and receiving of the Holy Communion, in the breaking of the Eucharist. . . . The usage of the primitive church was to have this daily (F.C. Cook, *The Bible Commentary*).

Celebrating the Lord's Supper. At first observed on the evening of every day . . . who also continued in the temple praising God and celebrating the Lord's Supper in their homes (*The Preachers Complete Homiletic Commentary*).

They continued steadfastly in the breaking of bread, i.e., in celebrating the sacrament of Lord's Supper, or Holy Comunion. At first the Lord's Supper was celebrated daily (*A Commentary of the Holy Bible* by various writers).

Breaking bread from house to house. They naturally observed their particular holy Rite, the Sacrament of the new covenant, apart from the public (*Commentary on the Holy Scriptures* by John Peter Lange).

These different Christian commentaries written by Biblical scholars all agree that the phrase *breaking of bread* refers to receiving Communion, the Eucharist or the Lord's Supper. All three terms identify the same sacred rite of receiving the bread and the fruit of the vine for the Communion meal.

Again, notice this was originally done "daily from house to house" (Acts 2:46).

As Often as You Do This

The Jewish Passover was celebrated once a year on the 14th of Nisan, which usually falls in the months of March or April. Christ was crucified at the season of Passover and introduced the New Covenant during this season.

Some Messianic believers teach the Communion should only be taken at Passover. However, the Bible says, "As oft as you do it" (1 Corinthians 11:24), which does not place a stipulation on a time frame or particular season.

The Communion meal was so important among the early church until it was conducted every day from house to house. I am positive that this was to ensure that the many believers scattered throughout a city would enjoy the personal and intimate fellowship with the Lord through His sacred meal among the faithful.

The Love Feasts

The New Testament also speaks of the love (agape) feasts. (Jude 12). The love feasts were a special feast hosted by the wealthier members of the church who provided a special meal for the poor in the congregations. Love feasts were for the poor, the widows, the orphans and others who lacked funds for their personal needs. Some scholars believe these were conducted every evening in connection with the Communion.

In the second century, the Agape Feast was separated from the Communion, and the two became separate rituals.

By the second century, when the Agape Feast was separated from the Communion, the Communion was conducted at the conclusion of the morning service, and the love feast later in the day.

According to historians, these feasts continued in the church until the fourth century, when they were banned by the Council of Laodicea. Some suggest that this act caused house-to-house Communion to be halted because it required believers to receive it only in the local churches.

No direct reference explains WHY the breaking of bread was moved from house-to-house, to an act solely in church facilities; but it appears to be that because the church grew, buildings were constructed in communities and cities where the believers met in local churches, instead of homes. Thus the local church became the heart of all spiritual activity, instead of the home.

Some suspect that the change, developed out of the church of Rome, was to prevent the common people from having any form of "spiritual authority" outside of the church hierarchy. By initiating the teaching that the Lord's Supper (called in Latin the Mass) could only be performed by a priest in the church, it forced the believers to be faithful in church attendance and to be under subjection to the spiritual "authority" of the local priests.

While the Bible does teach spiritual authority and believers being under subjection to those over you in the Lord (Hebrews 13:7), the Love Feasts were forgotten and the Lord's Supper became more of a weekly spiritual ritual to some, instead of an actual fellowship and healing meal in the intimacy of a believer's home.

Walking in Healing from the Beginning

We know that an important part of the Communion meal is healing through the atonement. In the earliest days of the church, it appears there was little physical sickness among its members. As hidden sin, disobedience, unforgiveness and strife entered the congregations, some became weak and sick. Others died prematurely.

This is clear from Paul's letter to the church at Corinth:

> For he who eats and drinks in an unworthy manner eats and drinks judgment to himself, not discerning the Lord's body. For this reason many are weak and sick among you, and many sleep (*1 Corinthians 11:29, 30*).

The early church "had all things common" (Acts 4:32). As long as believers walked in love (remember the love feasts?), centered their message on Christ and maintained a life of forgiveness, the members of the church fulfilled their days and grew in the grace of God.

The only negative Satanic force they encountered was persecution, which is guaranteed for those who live by the Word of God (Mark 4:17).

Today, as then, strife and envy in the church bring confusion and every evil work (James 3:16). Evil works open a door for the Enemy to work in the life of a believer. Living in contradiction to God's Word eventually leads to "giving place to the devil" (Ephesians 4:27).

The Church at Corinth

Some in the church at Corinth were opening the door to the devil. Paul wrote two separate, detailed letters to this church, the Books of 1 and 2 Corinthians. He began his first letter by exposing the well-known "secret" that the believers were not getting along well with each other. In fact there was "strife and division among them" (1 Corinthians 3:3).

He repeated this rebuke, telling them there were divisions and heresies among them (1 Corinthians 11:18). Because of this strife, many members were receiving the Lord's Supper in an "unworthy" fashion. It had stopped the healing flow of God from working among the people. Paul said:

> For this reason many are weak and sick among you, and many sleep [because you do not discern the body of Christ] (*1 Corinthians 11:30*).

As long as the church followed the simple revelation of Christ's atoning work and walked in pure love and faith, a continual manifestation of healing sealed their covenant. When "flesh" rose up, however, the result was weakness and sickness in the church.

This is why Paul instructed the believer to "examine himself" when receiving the Lord's Supper (1 Corinthians 11:28). The Greek word *examine* in this passage means "to test yourself." This inner searching turns the light on one's own flaws and weaknesses, causing a person to repent and confess his faults. This confessing of personal faults (*sins, missing the mark*), and praying for one another would lead to the blessing of healing.

> Confess your [faults] to one another, and pray for one another, that you may be healed. The effective, fervent prayer of a righteous man avails much (*James 5:16*).

Not Living by Bread Alone

It is not enough to receive just the bread of Communion in an act of faith. Jesus said, "Man shall not live by bread alone, but by every word of God" (Luke 4:4). It is important to receive your "daily bread" of God's Word through the bread of Communion, but you must also live by every Word that comes from the mouth of God!

For example, if you receive the bread of Communion, and in your heart you despise your brother, you are breaking the commandment of the New Covenant to love and forgive your enemies (Matthew 5:44). If you have not forgiven those who have wronged you and you want healing for yourself, you must first release the person you are holding hostage in your heart and forgive him his trespasses (Matthew 6:12). You cannot expect the healing power of God to work in your life if you are only eating the bread and not walking in obedience to the Word of God.

This is why we are to "confess our faults one to another" in order to be healed (James 5:16).

You cannot expect the healing power of God if you are only eating the bread and not walking in obedience to the Word of God.

Christ is our example. Before He died on the cross, He first prayed, "Father, forgive them; for they know not what they do" (Luke 23:34). Christ knew that he could not die to redeem mankind from sin if He himself died with unforgiveness toward those who had beaten and crucified Him. Even Stephen, while he was being stoned, asked God not to hold the sin of his death against those who murdered him (Acts 7:60).

Both of these prayers had amazing results. At the moment Christ died, a cruel centurion became a believer, saying, "Truly this was the Son of God" (Matthew 27:54). A man assisting in the stoning of Stephen was Saul of Tarsus, who was later converted and became the great apostle Paul (Acts 7:58).

Obedience to the Word includes not only understanding and participating in Communion, but also involves releasing anyone who has harmed us physically, emotionally or spiritually. This is how we judge ourselves at the Lord's Table—we examine our relationship with both God and man.

We can clearly see that breaking bread was a consistent, daily practice among the early Christians and was part of the Communion meal. We can also see that it was administered from house to house. The bread represented the precious body of our Lord, which was beaten for our healing (Isaiah 53:5; 1 Peter 2:24).

Scriptures reveal that this process of Christ's atoning work did not begin on the cross; it began in the garden of Gethsemane. Let us discover the secrets of redemption that began in the garden.

Secrets in the Garden of Gethsemane

And so it is written, "The first man Adam became a living being." The last Adam became a life-giving spirit (*1 Corinthians 15:45*).

✝ **The first Adam,** in the Garden of Eden, was not born through the natural birth process, but neither was **the second Adam,** Jesus Christ.

✝ **The first Adam** was formed from dust, and **the second Adam** was formed in the womb of a virgin (Genesis 2:7; Luke 1:27-31).

✝ **The first Adam** was perfect before the fall, and **the second Adam** was sinless throughout His life.

✝ **The first Adam** fell into sin while living in a garden called Eden, and **the second Adam** had the sins of the world placed on him in a garden called Gethsemane.

✝ **The first Adam** experienced death at the tree called "the knowledge of good and evil," the second Adam experienced death on a tree called a cross. **The second Adam**, through the Cross, conquered death, hell and the grave, however, and is alive for evermore (Revelation 1:18).

The redemptive process for mankind began, however, in a garden called Gethsemane. There is much mystery connected to Jesus' dark night in this garden. It was a favorite place for Him to go to reflect and pray (John 18:2).

Gethsemane was located between Jerusalem's Eastern Gate and the Mount of Olives. The Jerusalem Wall and the Mount of Olives were separated by the Kidron brook, a small stream of water flowing from beneath the city, eventually weaving through the mountains to the Dead Sea.

Some believe this garden may have been owned by Nicodemus or Joseph of Arimathea, both secret believers.

Christ entered the garden and invited three of his inner circle, Peter, James and John, to participate in an important late-night prayer meeting. Weary from previous events, the three chosen ones slept while Jesus interceded in fervent prayer. Christ knew what was coming. His prayer turned into an agonizing hour of intercession:

> And being in agony, He prayed more earnestly. Then His sweat became like great drops of blood falling down to the ground *(Luke 22:44).*

This could only happen under extreme stress as the blood capillaries expand and allow blood to mingle with the salty sweat. The word "agony" comes from the root word *agon,* which alludes to a contest or a fight.

The Cup

What was actually occurring? I believe this was the time when the sins of the world were being laid on Christ, just as in the Old Testament the sins were transferred to the scapegoat when the High Priest laid hands on the goat's head on the Day of Atonement.

This transfer of sins on Christ is alluded to in 2 Corinthians 5:21:

> For He made Him who knew no sin to be sin
> for us, that we might become the righteousness
> of God in Him (*2 Corinthians 5:21*).

> Him who knew no sin he made to be sin on
> our behalf; that we might become the
> righteousness of God in him (*ASV*).

As the sins of the world were placed on Christ, I believe He was experiencing the weight and burden of lost humanity. This agony appears to have lasted for three hours, as Christ requested that if possible, this "cup" pass from him (Matthew 26:42, 44). Paul wrote, indicating that this event almost physically killed Christ and he prayed to God to be spared from death:

> Who, in the days of His flesh, when He had
> offered up prayers and supplications, with
> vehement cries and tears to Him who was able
> to save Him from death, and was heard
> because of His godly fear, though He was a
> Son, yet He learned obedience by the things
> which He suffered (*Hebrews 5:7, 8*).

How did God "save Him from death," since Christ died on the cross the next day? God spared Christ from dying in the garden, as the pressure was causing his perspiration to become as drops of blood. This event was foreseen by Isaiah when he wrote, "[God] shall make His soul an *offering*" (Isaiah 53:10), and the prediction, "He shall bear their *iniquities*" (Isaiah 53:11). Further, Isaiah wrote about the suffering Messiah when he said:

> Surely He has borne our griefs and carried our sorrows; yet we esteemed Him stricken, smitten by God, and afflicted (*Isaiah 53:4*).

Over 600 years later, Matthew recalled this prophecy as being fulfilled through Jesus Christ when he saw Him healing the sick:

> He cast out the spirits with a word, and healed all who were sick, that it might be fulfilled which was spoken by Isaiah the prophet, saying: "He Himself took our infirmities and bore our sicknesses" (*Matthew 8:16, 17*).

The English Bible speaks of *griefs* and *sorrows* in Isaiah 53. Matthew, however, correctly translates these Hebrew words into *infirmities* and *sicknesses.* He reveals that Christ bore (carried in Him) our infirmities and sicknesses. Therefore, in the garden He was made sin with our sins and sick with our sicknesses. Is it any wonder He was praying for this "cup to pass?" Not for just the cup of the Cross, but He was praying for the sufferings He was experiencing at that moment.

Christ knew however, that this suffering would accomplish a future goal. He knew it would bring salvation and healing to those who would receive His New Covenant. This atonement would impact the bodies, souls and spirits of believers.

Body, Soul and Spirit

> May the God of peace Himself sanctify you completely; and may your whole spirit, soul, and body be preserved blameless at the coming of our Lord Jesus Christ (1 *Thessalonians 5:23*).

The physical body can become sick, the soul (mind) can experience negative emotions and the human spirit can become tainted by sin and disobedience to God. The atonement sets out to redeem the spirit, renew the soul and heal the body, and make a person whole, or complete, in Christ.

Isaiah breaks down how the sufferings of the Messiah will impact the tri-part nature of mankind.

1. The Atonement of the Body

> He has borne our griefs and carried our sorrows. . . . [B]y His stripes we are healed (*Isaiah 53:4, 5*).

2. The Atonement of the Soul

> He [was] despised and rejected by men, a Man of sorrows and acquainted with grief. He was oppressed and afflicted (*Isaiah 53:3, 7*).

3. The Atonement of the Spirit

> He was wounded for our transgressions, He was bruised for our iniquities. . . . [God shall] make His soul an offering for sin (*Isaiah 53:10*).

Three Men . . . Three Ministries of Atonement

It is no coincidence that Christ chose three disciples out of the Twelve to be His inner circle. The three-fold atonement of the body, soul and spirit can be illustrated in the lives and work of the three inner circle disciples.

✟   Peter: *Emotional* atonement (the mind)

✟   James: *Bodily* atonement

✟   John: *Spiritual* atonement

Peter and Emotional Healing

Peter certainly needed to renew his emotions. Before he received the Holy Spirit, the fellow was manipulated by his feelings and emotions.

✝   It was Peter who demanded to walk on water with Jesus (*Matthew 14:28*).

✝   Peter also rebuked Christ for predicting He would eventually die in Jerusalem (*Matthew 16:22*).

✝   The quick-spirited disciple also told Christ he would never deny him (*Matthew 26:33*).

✝   He whacked off a man's ear with a sword to prove his loyalty (*John 18:10*).

✝   Then a few hours later Peter was sitting by a night fire, cursing those who claimed he was a follower of Christ (*Matthew 26:69-75*).

Peter needed a complete overhaul of his emotions before he would be stable enough to become a true leader in the church.

James and Physical Healing

James is the writer who penned instructions for praying for the sick in the church:

> Is anyone among you sick? Let him call for the elders of the church, and let them pray over him, anointing him with oil in the name of

the Lord. And the prayer of faith will save the sick, and the Lord will raise him up. And if he has committed sins, he will be forgiven. Confess your trespasses to one another, and pray for one another, that you may be healed. The effective, fervent prayer of a righteous man avails much (*James 5:14-16*).

This passage in James deals primarily with the physical aspect of healing, and not just spiritual healing. The prayer of the elders is for a believer in the church. The sick are to "call for the elders." The emphasis is to first confess your faults, your trespasses, in order to be healed. James deals with the physical aspect of healing.

John and the Healing of the Spirit

The third disciple, John, is a picture of the atonement of the human spirit. John's Gospel is the main Biblical writing that ministers use when instructing converts to read and understand the ministry as well as the redemptive plan of Christ.

John gives the most details concerning the atoning work of Christ from the Garden of Gethsemane to the Cross and the Resurrection. He was the only disciple with direct access to the trial and crucifixion of Christ (John 18:16; 19:27).

These three men represent the three aspects of what Christ's redemptive work would do for humanity: it would provide healing of the body, soul and spirit.

Mysteries in the Garden

Not only was sin and sickness being placed on God's Lamb, Jesus Christ, but Satan was also interested in the activity taking place in Gethsemane. Jesus made this clear in John 14:30, when He was preparing for the conflict in the garden:

> I will no longer talk much with you, for the ruler of this world is coming, and he has nothing in Me. . . . Arise, let us go from here (*John 14:30, 31*).

The ruler of this world was Satan himself. Christ wanted His disciples to know that what they were about to see was not Satan defeating him, but a plan of God from the foundation of the world (Colossians 1:26). This plan had been hid from ages past; but when Christ came, it was about to be made known. It was a mystery to Satanic powers, however:

> None of the rulers of this age knew; for had they known, they would not have crucified the Lord of glory (*1 Corinthians 2:8*).

This passage indicates that Satan would have stopped Christ's death had he known the full impact it would have on the devil's dark kingdom.

When Judas entered the garden with a band of Roman soldiers (600) to seize Christ, the Savior was now prepared to be the sin offering for the world (John 18:1-3). From this garden near the ancient Temple, the Son of God went to offer Himself as God's final Lamb who would take away the sin of the world.

Sin came on Adam in the Garden of Eden and sin was placed on Christ in the garden of Gethsemane. It was not *His* sins; rather, it was the sins of others that He would carry to the cross.

Jesus made no distinction between forgiveness for the soul and healing for the body.

Jesus was a substitute for us. He carried both our *diseases* and our *sins*. Many churches emphasize the forgiveness of sins evident throughout the Bible and especially in the ministry of Jesus; but He made no distinction between forgiveness and physical healing. In fact, healing and forgiveness went hand in hand.

Christ told a man, "Your sins are forgiven." Then He commanded, "Rise, take up your bed and walk" (Matthew 9:1-7). James said when a believer is healed, "If he has committed sins, he will be forgiven" (James 5:15).

In Gethsemane Christ revealed to Nicodemus that as Moses lifted the serpent in the wilderness, so He (Christ) would be lifted up (on the cross) to draw all men to Him (John 3:14).

The story of the brass serpent is again a picture of the redemptive work of Christ. Israel had sinned, and the people were bitten by serpents. As they lay dying, Moses constructed a brass serpent on a pole. All who looked to the brass snake lived (Numbers 21)! God chose a brass serpent to represent Christ, since brass represents humanity and the serpent represents sin. Christ became a human and took sin upon Himself to the cross!

Other symbolism is used to represent Christ and His atoning work. Another dynamic picture is the manna that fell from heaven in the wilderness. This angels' food (Psalm 78:25) sustained Israel during their 40 years in the wilderness.

Jesus himself said: "Moses did not give you the bread from heaven, but My Father gives you the true bread from heaven. For the bread of God is He who comes down from heaven and gives life to the world" (John 6:5, 10). We will look at the manna in the wilderness and the Bread from God in the next chapter.

The Mystery of the Manna

Then Jesus said to them, "Most assuredly, I say to you, Moses did not give you the bread from heaven, but My Father gives you the true bread from heaven" *(John 6:32)*.

God provided supernatural nourishment for over 600,000 men and their families, as they wandered through the wilderness for 40 years (Exodus 12:37; 16:35). For six days a week, a supernatural bread from heaven, called *manna*, fell on the ground during the night, like dew (Numbers 11:9).

There is something of a mystery about this manna which Israel ate in the wilderness. It is called the "bread from heaven" and "angels' food" (Psalms 78:25). When Israel saw the small white wafers lying on the ground they called it "manna." The root word for manna in Hebrew is *mah*, which simply means *what*.

So when the children of Israel saw it, they said to one another, "What is it?" For they did not know what it was (Exodus 16:15).

> And the house of Israel called its name Manna. And it was like white coriander seed, and the taste of it was like wafers made with honey (*Exodus 16:31*).

> The manna was like coriander seed, and its color like the color of bdellium (*Numbers 11:7*).

These Scriptures reveal the following facts about Manna:

- ✞ Manna was something Israel had never seen before.
- ✞ Manna had the texture of a wafer.
- ✞ Manna had a slight taste of honey.
- ✞ Manna was similar to a coriander seed.
- ✞ Manna fell during the night.
- ✞ Manna was the color of bdellium, pearly white.

Manna had to be eaten daily to sustain the people and give them strength for their journey. In the New Testament, Jesus compared Himself to this manna in the wilderness. He announced that He was the true bread come down from heaven:

> Then Jesus said to them, "Most assuredly, I say to you, Moses did not give you the bread from heaven, but My Father gives you the true bread from heaven" (*John 6:32*).

In the Communion supper, the bread is a representation of the physical body of Christ. The Bible says, "He was wounded for our transgressions, He was bruised for our iniquities" (Isaiah 53:5). These wounds and bruises were physical marks placed on Christ when He endured the literal whipping prior to His crucifixion. These bruises were laid on His back, and provided for our healing (Isaiah 53:5).

Other wounds were caused by nails piercing His hands and feet. The gaping wound in His side was caused by a spear. The bruises and stripes on His body were caused by a violent beating with an object called a cat-of-nine-tails, a short handled whip with nine long, leather straps, each embedded with pieces of metal at the end.

The Jewish bread used during Passover today is a perfect picture of the body of Christ. Called matzo bread, it is square-shaped and white in color, with long rows and holes piercing the bread. The bread has no leaven (which represents sin), and is slightly browned on the surface.

Matzo bread, used by Jews today for Passover, is a perfect picture of the body of Christ. . . .

Lines running across the bread form a picture of the furrows placed in the back of Christ; the holes symbolize the piercing in His hands, feet and side; and the brown spots allude to the bruises on His body.

The Manna Was Beaten

Before the manna was eaten and the people received nourishment from the heavenly bread, it was necessary for the manna to be beaten and crushed:

The people went about and gathered it, ground it on millstones or beat it in the mortar, cooked it in pans, and made cakes of it; and its taste was like the taste of pastry prepared with oil (Numbers 11:8).

Once the manna was beaten it could also be baked in a pan. It takes a fire, or heat, to bake something. Just as the manna was beaten in order to be eaten, so the body of Christ was beaten in order that we could receive His body through the bread of the Lord's table!

The Coriander Seed

The manna was compared to a coriander seed. I was unfamiliar with the coriander until an interview I conducted with Dr. John Miller. This seed is from a plant with which the Egyptians were familiar. Dr. Miller pointed out something I had not noticed before.

A normal coriander seed looks like it has some form of stripe running across each one. The interesting aspect is that what looks like stripes are, in reality, small furrows on the outer shell.

It is interesting how the manna in the wilderness relates to the coriander seed. The tiny seed itself speaks loudly to us of how Christ was beaten until there were marks and lines imprinted on His body! "The plowers plowed on my back; they made their furrows long" (Psalm 129:3).

The Hoar Frost on the Ground

When the manna appeared on the ground, it looked like a "hoar frost" covering the ground.

> And when the dew that lay was gone up, behold, upon the face of the wilderness there lay a small round thing, as small as the hoar frost on the ground (*Exodus 16:14*).

The phrase *hoar frost* is an unusual phrase. The root word in Hebrew is *kephowr,* a word which is akin to the Hebrew word *kippur.* "Yom Kippur" is the Hebrew phrase meaning the Day of Atonement. The word *atonement,* which is mentioned 80 times in the Hebrew Bible, is the word *kippur.* Its meaning is "to cover, to appease and to purge."

The word describes what occurred once a sacrifice was offered to God. The blood offering was an atonement offering for sins and transgressions.

How unique it was that manna fell from heaven, covering the ground like a frost. It anticipated the coming of Christ and His influence in the earth. It was as though God was looking ahead in time to when the true Bread from heaven, Christ, would come down and spill His blood on the ground to atone for humanity!

The True Bread

Just as the Hebrews ate manna and were sustained by it, when we eat the bread from heaven through the Communion Supper, we are receiving in our own body His strength, His life, His peace, His righteousness and the healing He provides.

In John 6, Christ spoke of manna from Moses' time, and stated that He himself was the true bread from heaven.

> I tell you for certain that Moses wasn't the one who gave you bread from heaven. My Father is the one who gives you the true bread from heaven. And the bread that God gives is the one who came down from heaven to give life to the world (*John 6:32, 33*).

He was responding to their complaint that unlike Jesus feeding the multitude one meal, Moses had fed Israel with manna on a regular basis. That's when Jesus made this astonishing statement:

> Whoever eats My flesh and drinks My blood has eternal life, and I will raise him up at the last day. For My flesh is food indeed, and My blood is drink indeed. He who eats My flesh and drinks My blood abides in Me, and I in him (*John 6:54-56*).

When Christ made this statement in the synagogue, the crowds began to leave, shaking their heads and questioning His saying. They were not aware that this was a prophecy concerning how we could receive the life of the body and blood of Christ through Communion.

The Fruit of the Vine

When the Bible speaks of wine, most people visualize a wine bottle in a restaurant. In the Bible, however, the word *wine* is used even when the grapes are still on the vine. The Old Testament has two Hebrew words for wine, one identifying fermented and the other unfermented wine.

In the New Testament, there is only one main Greek word (*oinos*) used for wine, and this makes it difficult to distinguish between fermented and unfermented wine. It is interesting, however, that when Christ held up the cup He called it the "fruit of the vine" (Matthew 26:29; Mark 14:25; Luke 22:18).

This seems to indicate the juice in the cup was fresh juice, and not wine that had been fermented to a point that made it intoxicating. Also, it was common during a Jewish Passover to mix three parts water to one part wine, so there would be no effect from any alcohol content.

The bread used in Passover and at the Communion is to have no leaven in it. This is because leaven is a picture of sin (1 Corinthians 5:7, 8). Since Christ was sinless, His blood would have been un-tainted by Adam's sin na-ture. Thus, fermented wine was a picture of sin in the blood. This is why I believe pure "blood of the grape," or pure juice, is the best choice to use in Communion.

Christ also identifies Himself as the "true vine" (John 15:1). Since He is the true vine *and* the true bread from heaven, then the pure blood of the grape represents His sinless blood and the unleavened bread is a symbol of His holy body.

Since He is the true vine and the true bread from heaven, then the blood of the grape represents His sinless blood and the bread is a symbol of His holy body. . . .

The Table of Showbread

Another picture of "holy" bread is the table of showbread. In both the Tabernacle of Moses and in

Solomon's Temple, one of the sacred pieces of furniture was the golden table which held 12 loaves of bread. This golden table was positioned in the second chamber, the inner court or Holy Place, against the northern wall, or curtain.

Each week the priest prepared the bread by sifting fine flour and baking 12 loaves of bread, representing the 12 tribes of Israel. Each Sabbath, the priest would eat from this table and the bread would be replaced for another week.

The bread was also identified as the "bread of face," because the table was close to the veil, the dividing curtain between the Holy Place and the Holy of Holies. Not only were there 12 tribes, but during a normal year there were 12 months. This again pictures the necessity of eating bread on a weekly basis throughout the year.

Because the Manna was eaten every day in the wilderness and Christ was a picture of the Manna, then the Manna should be received every day. We can, and must, receive our spiritual nourishment through the written Word, the *Rhema* (quickened) Word, and by receiving the body of Christ through Communion.

The Priesthood of the Believer

But you are a chosen generation, a royal priesthood, a holy nation, His own special people, that you may proclaim the praises of Him who called you out of darkness into His marvelous light *(1 Peter 2:9).*

To this day, some older Christian denominations continue the practice of conducting their weekly services with the older traditions that have been passed down for centuries. If a believer, however, begins to examine when, where and how these traditions emerged, he gets the idea that much of the liturgy was developed out of the culture of that day and not so much from the Holy Scriptures themselves.

The Jewish linkage of the Communion Meal to the Jewish Passover was lost in the church by the fourth century. The Council of Nicea said in 325, "It appeared an unworthy thing that in this celebration of this most holy feast we should follow the practice of the Jews."

Two results can be seen in how the Roman church views the priesthood and the idea of saints. In order to be placed in the high position of a saint in the Roman system, a person has to have a long list of qualifications and a documented miracle during his or her lifetime.

The New Testament however, calls all believers who are actively serving God, "saints." The New Testament Greek word for "saints" is *hagios*, meaning to be "morally blameless and spiritually consecrated to God." The word *saint* is used 61 times in the New Testament. Paul says the "saints greet you" in several of his letters (Romans 16:15; 2 Corinthians 13:13; Philippians 4:22; Hebrews 13:24).

When a believer in Christ begins to walk in full obedience to God's Word and begins to consecrate himself to God morally and spiritually, he becomes marked as a saint of the Lord.

Kings and Priests

The second issue is the role of priests. My great grand-father came from Italy, and was very familiar with the Roman priesthood. Many of the priests are men who have dedicated their lives to God and taken a vow not to marry or to gather personal wealth.

The one element that I have observed, however, is that so many of the rituals are based on the Old Testament concept of approaching God instead of the New Testament revelation under the New Covenant.

For example, some are taught that they must confess to an earthly priest in order to be forgiven of sins. This is an Old Testament concept. The New Testament teaches that the Lord Jesus Christ is our High Priest, and we ourselves are to come boldly before God's throne to be forgiven (Hebrews 4:16).

While many Christians look to a single individual as the spiritual leader, the New Testament concept is that each believer is a part of a larger, universal priesthood. The revelation as individual believers as priests is revealed to John in the Book of Revelation:

> And has made us kings and priests to His
> God and Father, to Him be glory and

dominion forever and ever. Amen *(Revelation 1:6).*

Every believer is a priest unto God. No priest or minister on earth has the power to forgive sins, however. Only Christ can forgive sins, because He paid the price to forgive sins by His death. We need no human mediator, since our Mediator is sitting on God's right hand.

The people who do not accept this Biblical revelation are usually those who have no confidence in their own prayers and feel an unworthiness to ask God for forgiveness. As priests unto God, we are to offer sacrifices of praise, give our offerings, minister to the Lord and help bring people into the grace and knowledge of Christ's redemption.

In the Old Testament the priests were permitted to eat each week, the 12 loaves of bread which were prepared on the table of showbread. This bread was replaced weekly with fresh bread.

Who Serves the Lord's Table?

Most Protestant denominations offer ordination to faithful ministers who fulfill detailed requirements for the office of Bishop. For example, I am ordained as a Bishop in a major denomination. As a bishop I am permitted to conduct the Lord's Supper in a local service, baptize believers, serve on major boards and be elected to higher positions within the church.

Some ordained ministers are too restrictive in their belief that only a fellow ordained minister who has an "official" ordination should perform the Communion supper.

It is certainly important for the body of believers to participate in the Communion meal with their local church and minister. We

The priests were permitted to eat from the 12 loaves on the table of showbread.

must also understand, however, the New Testament concept of individual believers being priests.

God does call certain people to teach, to pastor churches and to evangelize the world. This is part of the five-fold ministry for the "perfecting of the saints." No part of the New Testament states, however, that an "ordained minister" must be the one to conduct the Lord's Supper. Paul gives a list of requirements for a bishop:

> This is a faithful saying: If a man desires the
> position of a bishop, he desires a good work.
> A bishop then must be blameless, the husband
> of one wife, temperate, sober-minded, of good
> behavior, hospitable, able to teach; not given
> to wine, not violent, not greedy for money,
> but gentle, not quarrelsome, not covetous;
> one who rules his own house well, having
> his children in submission with all reverence
> (for if a man does not know how to rule his
> own house, how will he take care of the
> church of God?); not a novice, lest being
> puffed up with pride he fall into the same
> condemnation as the devil. Moreover he
> must have a good testimony among those
> who are outside, lest he fall into reproach
> and the snare of the devil (*1 Timothy 3:1-7*).

I believe the Roman church committed a great error when it decided to move the Communion supper from being allowed in the home, and decreed that it was to be conducted strictly in the local church. While the church is the focal point for community worship, the home is the focus for personal and individual worship.

As a fourth generation minister, I strongly believe the local church should have a gathering in which the pastor hosts the sacred supper for the local assembly. Jesus did not place a specific time or location in which to enjoy communion with Him, however. He said, "As often as you do this" (see 1 Corinthians 11:25).

Your Body is the Temple

During the time of Moses, the tabernacle was constructed as a dwelling place for God. Once Israel seized the Promised Land, a permanent structure, the Temple, was erected in Jerusalem. Both of these sacred edifices had an outer court, an inner court and a holy of holies.

After Christ's Resurrection, however, the sacrifices at the earthly Temple became a useless ritual because Christ was the final offering for sin and guilt.

The same can be said of the Temple. God changed His earthly dwelling place from a building made with men's hands to human beings made in His image. Paul wrote that our body is "the Temple of God and . . . the Spirit of God dwells in you" (1 Corinthians 3:16).

The earthly Temple needed repairs and special upkeep on a consistent basis. A lamb was offered in the morning and in the evening of each day. Since our body is the temple of God, the outer court represents our physical body, the inner court represents our soul and the Holy of Holies represents our spirit. The blood of the lamb in the morning and evening alludes to our need of being "covered by Christ's blood" in the morning when we begin our day and in the evening when we conclude our day.

The priesthood was responsible for the care of the Temple just as you and I are responsible for the care of our bodies, our souls and our spirits. Under the Old Covenant God would not let certain types of animals enter the congregation of the Lord. He also laid down certain restrictions for the Levites, priests and the high priest concerning moral and spiritual conduct in the holy house.

God was so concerned about the health of His people that He gave guidelines regarding food to eat. Many times believers are careless about how they treat their temple. We eat food that is not healthy, we seldom exercise and we allow fear, worry and stress to weigh us down.

This combination is unhealthy and can shorten our days. After the body is a physical wreck, people often want an instant miracle to get everything out of order back in order. This is why it is important to understand that Communion is a holy and sacred act, not some get-healed-quick, magic formula.

Communion Is a Covenant, not a Magic Formula

For this is My blood of the new covenant, which is shed for many for the remission of sins *(Matthew 26:28).*

When Doctor Miller and I started airing Manna-Fest programs on receiving Communion, I began receiving letters from various individuals who did not quite understand the spiritual significance and importance of the Communion process.

There were a few (and I do mean very few) who seemed to view the Communion as some sort of "magic formula." These people were often young in their knowledge of the Lord or were persons with little, if any, Christian training and Biblical knowledge.

Americans are noted for trying the latest fad or indulging the latest formula. We purchase the most recent workout equipment, hoping to solve the problem of the ever-growing "love handles" that keep expanding on our hips. We then attempt the "revolutionary diet" recently tested and proven among the heaviest Americans, who now testify of how this "breakthrough" melted excess pounds like jelly in hot water.

We must not treat the sacred time with Christ and the Communion as the secular marketers do some get-rich-quick success program, however. The Communion meal is part of the Covenant relationship between God and His children!

Abraham, the Example

Abraham is considered the Father of all who are in the faith (Romans 4:16). When he was returning from battle with the five kings, he traveled to Jerusalem (called Salem in that day). He went to meet Melchizedek, the first king and priest of the Most High God (Genesis 14).

In the Valley of Shaveh, today the Kidron Valley, Abraham received bread and wine from Melchizedek. This was a "covenant meal" during which Melchizedek blessed Abraham and where God reconfirmed Abraham's promise of a son who would become a great nation (Genesis 15:1-4).

At a "covenant meal" shared by Abraham and Melchizedek, God confirmed the promise He had made to Abraham.

Melchizedek is a mysterious person in both Hebrew tradition and Christian theology. The Jews teach that Melchizedek was not the man's name, but a title given to him. The name comes from two Hebrew words: *Melech*, which means "king" and *zadok*, which means "righteousness."

He was king of *Salem*, a word translated "peace" in Hebrew (Genesis 14:18). Jews believe he was actually Shem, the righteous son of Noah, who settled in this area to teach righteousness and reveal that the Messiah would appear from his linage.

The New Testament indicates that Jesus became the true High Priest over the Temple of God in heaven and is the true Messiah. The priesthood of Christ is patterned after the priesthood of Melchizedek:

> Though He was a Son, yet [Jesus] learned obedience by the things which He suffered. And having been perfected, He became the author of eternal salvation to all who obey Him, called by God as High Priest "according to the order of Melchizedek" *(Hebrews 5:8-10).*

Among the priests of ancient Israel, Aaron was the first to minister in the Tabernacle of Moses. Jewish sources indicate that about 86 High Priests may have ministered from Aaron until the destruction of Herod's Temple in A.D. 70.

In David's time a man named Zadok was the High Priest and was faithful to David during his most difficult times. Therefore, the priesthood of the future kingdom of Israel was promised to the sons of Zadok for their faithfulness (Ezekiel 48:8-11).

Why was Christ's priesthood compared to Melchizedek's and not Aaron's or Zadok's? Aaron and Zadok were strictly priests of God; this was their only role. Melchizedek however, was both a king and a priest of the Most High God (Hebrews 7:1).

Christ is presently in the heavenly Temple serving as our High Priest (Hebrews 4:14; 8:1, 2). When He returns to earth, however, he will rule and reign as King of kings (Revelation 19:16). As Melchizedek was king and priest in Jerusalem, giving forth the bread and wine of the covenant, so Christ is our king and priest with whom we have an eternal covenant. And we will reign with Him from Jerusalem during a thousand-year kingdom on earth (Revelation 20:4).

The Power of the Covenant

God takes very serious the Covenants He makes with men. In fact there are several major covenants mentioned in the Bible:

The Person	The Covenant Promise
The Noachian Covenant	*The earth would never again be destroyed by water.*
The Abrahamic Covenant	*His son would produce a nation that would rule other nations.*
The Davidic Covenant	*David would rule from Jerusalem as king forever.*
The New Covenant	*We can receive eternal life through Christ.*

In the Abrahamic Covenant, the sign a Jewish male had "cut the covenant" with God was the physical act of circumcision. Every male child was circumcised in the flesh of his foreskin on the eighth day of his life. This rite was a token that he would be raised to believe in the God of Abraham, and that he would be raised in a covenant relationship (Genesis 17:11-12).

After Christ's resurrection, the new Gentile believers had no need of this rite because circumcision was no longer in the flesh of a man but in the heart, or the nature, of man. In the New Covenant, water baptism now replaces the physical act of circumcision:

> In Him you were also circumcised with the circumcision made without hands, by putting off the body of the sins of the flesh, by the circumcision of Christ, buried with Him in baptism, in which you also were raised with Him through faith in the working of God, who raised Him from the dead *(Colossians 2:11, 12)*.

The Bible teaches that if you repent and be baptized, you will be saved (Mark 16:16). Under the Old Covenant, if a Jewish child was not circumcised he would be cut off from among the people (Genesis 17:14). If a person does not repent and be baptized according to the Scripture, he cannot be saved (Acts 2:38).

Water baptism identifies you publicly as a believer in Christ. It is a picture of you being buried in Christ and coming up out of the water with a new life. In the early church, baptism immediately followed a person's conversion to Christ (Acts 2:38; Acts 8:12; Acts 8:38; Acts 9:18; 10:48; 16:15; 18:8; 19:5; 22:17). Water baptism should be emphasized the moment a person comes to Christ.

Communion, however, identifies you as an intimate believer in Christ. Only a member of the family of God can partake in the Lord's Supper. Otherwise, the person receiving it is receiving it unworthily.

The Prayer of Faith and the Communion Meal

When I began to understand the spiritual truth of the power of Communion, one of the most important areas of illumination was how powerful Communion is as it relates to faith and healing. There are many methods of healing found in Scripture. There is healing by speaking the Word, healing through a manifestation of the Spirit and healing through the gifts of the Spirit.

In the church, however, the most common method is the prayer of faith. We are told "the prayer of faith will save the sick, and the Lord will raise him up" (James 5:15).

During a prayer of faith, unbelief, or the lack of faith, can actually become a hindrance to the prayer being answered.

A person must believe in the power of Christ's body and blood, and that its redemptive anointing is working to produce healing and strength. . . .

A person's faith may be stronger on some occasions than at other times; and as humans, we often judge the power of our prayers on the circumstances or feelings surrounding the request.

For example, the human mind reasons that a headache is nothing for God to heal, but terminal cancer is another story. In many of the methods of healing, however, the manifestation comes as a result of the person's faith.

The same is true with Communion. A person must believe in the healing power of Christ's body and blood, and that the redemptive anointing of Christ is working in his body to produce healing and strength. Faith is the path all spiritual blessings follow.

Communion is powerful because it is based on God's Covenant with us. Actually, when I receive Communion I sense such a relief in knowing that I am leaning, not on another person's prayers or another's faith, but I am simply trusting in the covenant!

This takes the pressure off of a person. It relieves the pressure that he or she must have a stronger faith, a special atmosphere or a greater anointing to see a manifestation of healing.

Healing Crusades and Conferences

In the 1940s and 1950s, numerous men operated in the gifts of healing and miracles (1 Corinthians 12:7-10). Multitudes attended these meetings and many were healed of numerous sicknesses and diseases.

My father recalls how people would say, "If I can just get to the big tent of Brother So-and-So, I will be healed." Many times they were healed because they released their faith, not in the man, but in the anointing that was present when he prayed for the sick.

In those days the crowds would be from 5,000 to 15,000 a night. The minister would often sit in a chair and personally pray for each person who wanted healing, for hours. The minister would become weary; but if anyone was missed in the prayer line, the seeker left disappointed.

Conversely, some attend healing meetings today and leave disappointed because the minister didn't call them out or the Lord didn't seem to have his eye on them.

Secular unbelievers often mock these meetings and consider them a sham or a show designed to get recognition and bilk people out of a few dollars in the offerings. This causes stress on those ministers who walk in this calling, because the sincere ones have a burden for people and are often accused of being fake—all because someone was prayed for and wasn't healed.

One great minister in the 1940s was told by a skeptical preacher, "If you can really heal the sick, go to the local hospital and pray for them to be healed. Empty out the intensive care unit."

The man answered, "You are a preacher. Why don't you go to the hospital and win them all to the Lord. Get everyone saved if you believe in salvation."

The skeptic replied, "A person must believe in order to be saved."

The healing minister replied, "And a person must believe in order to be healed!"

Others seeking healing often believe that a certain atmosphere must be created in order to ensure the healing prayer will work. This may be true with some ministers, because they feel they cannot function in an "anointing" unless the stage, the music and the lighting are just right. But this is not a requirement for the power of God.

God *does* use people to minister to others; He *does* bring special miracles through the anointing of His Spirit (Acts 19:11). I believe the most perfect way of receiving anything from the Lord, however, is through your *own personal faith* in the Word. This is why Communion is so powerful.

God is true to His covenant. He is true to His Word. David praised God because "You have magnified Your word above all Your name" (Psalms 138:2). God is so true to His covenant that when He intended to destroy Israel for worshiping the golden calf, Moses simply reminded God of His covenant with Abraham, and the "Lord repented" of His decision to destroy Israel (Exodus 32:14).

Acting out Your Faith

Faith without works, or action, is dead (James 2:26). Before Christ healed the sick, He often required the person to perform an act of faith to demonstrate that he or she was believing for the miracle. Incidents are numerous. For example, Jesus said:

> "Stretch forth thy hand" to a man with a withered hand (*Luke 6:10*).
>
> "Go show yourself to the priests" to 10 lepers (*Luke 5:14*).
>
> "Take up your bed and walk" to a paralyzed man (*John 5:8*).
>
> "Go wash in the pool of Siloam" to a blind man (*John 9:7*).

Years ago a gifted evangelist had great results ministering to the sick. Before prayer he would tell folks to act out their faith by doing what they *can* do — move a part of their body or begin praising God in advance.

A young girl who had been in an accident was paralyzed from the neck down. She began rolling her eyes up and down as a sign of her faith that God would touch her. The minister saw her and knew what she was doing. She was acting on her faith in the only manner she could, moving the only thing she could move—her eyes.

As he prayed for her, the power of God shot through her body, and she was able to stand up and walk. She eventually began running and praising God. Her mother was so shocked she fainted! Faith is vitally necessary, but faith must be accompanied by action.

By taking the time to prepare the Communion supper and by spending time meditating on Christ and His covenant, you are acting on your faith. You would not take time to go through the process if you did not consider the act to be of great importance to your life.

God loves to see His people act out their faith. He loves it when we understand His covenant. The Bible says:

> My covenant will I not break, nor alter the thing that is gone out of my lips (*Psalms 89:34*).

Relying on God's Promises

The Old Testament covenant was based on obedience to the written Law of God, as recorded in the five books of Moses called the Torah. The New Covenant is based on an individual walking in repentance and forgiveness, and acting on the promises given in the New Testament.

Paul taught that we have a "better covenant . . . established on better promises" (Hebrews 8:6). A promise, by definition, is a "divine assurance of something good." Here are a few of the *many promises* given to believers in the New Testament:

✝   Salvation by faith (*Ephesians 2:8*)

✝   Justification by faith (*Romans 5:1*)

✝   The promise of the Holy Spirit (*Acts 2:39*)

✝   The promise of healing (*1 Peter 2:24*)

✝   The promise of Christ's return (*Acts 1:11*)

✝   The promise of heaven (*John 14:1, 2*)

✝   The promise of eternal life (*John 3:14-17*)

✝   The promise of ruling with Christ (*Revelation 20:6*)

Receiving Communion is both an act of faith and an act of obedience. God is moved toward us when He sees us act on our faith in His Word. He is pleased when He sees us believing the words of His Covenant. Jesus said it this way:

> If you abide in Me, and My words abide in
> you, you will ask what you desire, and it shall
> be done for you (*John 15:7*).

The Communion is in proportion to our faith. When a person partakes with no faith, there is no communion. The message of the Communion meal is that Jesus' sacrificial death is our spiritual life and nourishment.

The Holy Spirit uses this message to strengthen our faith in such a way that we have a spiritual communion with the total person of Jesus.

The Holy Spirit accomplishes for us what the Lord's Supper symbolizes. Our bodies are nourished and healed through the earthly bread and wine, but our souls are nourished and healed through the heavenly body and blood.

The Holy Spirit seeks to minister life and blessing to an area where death once reigned, and this is the message of the cup. The Spirit seeks to lead us into all righteousness in an area where sin once reigned, and this is the message of the bread.

When we partake of the bread by faith, we are utilizing the power of His sacrifice. We are taking advantage of the price He paid. We are exercising authority over curses such as want, poverty and sickness. We are taking authority over the works of the devil who seeks to kill, steal and destroy.

We drink the cup by faith, as well as eat the bread by faith. The cup represents the blood of Christ that wars against Satan for us. We overcome the enemy by His blood (Revelation 12:11). Drinking the cup in faith means that we are drinking God's rich promises of provision for our every need. By faith we are receiving all of God's nourishment, provision and support.

The best news of all is that when we commemorate His death and His sacrifice through Communion, we are anticipating that heavenly banquet when we "drink it new" with Him in the Father's Kingdom. We'll talk about that banquet in the next chapter.

The *Didache* and the

Messianic Banquet

Then he said to me, "Write: 'Blessed are those who are called to the marriage supper of the Lamb!'" And he said to me, "These are the true sayings of God" (*Revelation 19:9*).

Christ was born in Bethlehem. The word Bethlehem comes from two Hebrew words, *beyth*, meaning house and *lechem*, meaning bread. The meaning of Bethlehem is, therefore, the *house of bread*.

The beautiful story of Ruth and Boaz unfolded in Bethlehem. Ruth, a Moabite (a Gentile), followed her mother-in-law, Naomi, from Moab back to her home city of Bethlehem. Ruth, a widow, gleaned in the fields of a rich Jew named Boaz. Ruth gained the favor of the rich, single landowner, and eventually married him. From the bloodline of Ruth and Boaz came David, the promised king of Israel (Ruth 4:21, 22).

When Boaz died, his son, Obed, inherited his fields. After Obed's death, the land was passed to *his* son, Jesse, the father of David. These fields grew both barley and wheat. During the time of the Jewish Temple, the grain from the fields of Bethlehem was harvested to make bread at the Temple, including the bread baked for the table of showbread.

Centuries later, in this same town of Bethlehem the true Bread from heaven was born, Jesus the Messiah!

Special Meals among the Jews

Some scholars believe that the concept of a "Communal Meal" may have originated with a group called the Essenes. This secluded group of men lived in the Judean Wilderness, close to the Dead Sea. They are noted for preserving the famous Dead Sea Scrolls in jars and hiding them in caves for future generations.

They were a very mystical group who believed in the future redemption of Israel and a Messiah who would redeem the nation. According to scholars, the Essenes would wash in water, put on white garments and gather in their assembly hall. They would bless the bread and then the wine.

Because the fruit of the vine represents the sinless blood of Christ, unfermented juice should be used. . . .

The wine was actually "young sweet wine before it was fermented." The same procedure of blessing is followed in Christian Communion. Believers assemble together, having been cleansed of their sins and given "white garments" (representing the righteousness of the saints), and they bless the bread and the fruit of the vine.

Because the fruit of the vine (juice) represents the sinless blood of Christ, pure unfermented juice should be used. Fermented wine contains decay. This is similar to leaven in bread which, in the Bible, represents sin. It is interesting that Jesus washed the feet of his disciples *prior* to the last supper.

Another example of the Communal Meal is a group of Egyptian Jewish ascetics in the first century who were called *Therapeutae* (Greek for "healers"). They settled near Alexandria, Egypt, and lived a life of separation similar to the Essenes, according to Philo. Some scholars believe this group of was an offshoot of the Essenes, in the pre-Christian era.

This group spent most of their time in prayer and study. They read the Torah, the prophets and the Psalms. For six days they lived in solitude, never leaving the main house. On the seventh day, however, both men and women met in a large, divided sanctuary where they ate a special Communal Meal consisting of spring water and bread flavored with hyssop or salt.

The group avoided wine and meat. Following the meal, a special, sacred vigil continued until dawn.

The Communal Meal of the Essenes, however, was considered a preview of the final Messianic meal to be eaten with the Messiah at the end of days. According to New Testament writers, the Communion Meal is closely connected to the Passover Meal, called the *seder*. Conducted by the Jews each year, it reminds them of their deliverance from Egyptian bondage.

During this season, Christ introduced the New Covenant of His body and His blood to the disciples. Scripture teaches that the Communion supper does "proclaim the Lord's death till He comes" (1 Corinthians 11:26).

At the final Passover meal, Jesus took the fourth cup, called the cup of consummation, and introduced it as the "cup of the Kingdom." When He returns for the church and resurrects the dead in Christ, He will initiate us into the Kingdom of heaven; and at the Marriage Supper of the Lamb, He will "consummate" the marriage with His bride.

> And I heard, as it were, the voice of a great multitude, as the sound of many waters and as the sound of mighty thunderings, saying, "Alleluia! For the Lord God Omnipotent reigns! Let us be glad and rejoice and give Him glory, for the marriage of the Lamb has come, and His wife has made herself ready." And to her it was granted to be arrayed in fine linen, clean and bright, for the fine linen is the righteous acts of the saints. Then he said to me, "Write: 'Blessed are those who

are called to the marriage supper of the Lamb!'" And he said to me, "These are the true sayings of God" (*Revelation 19:6-9*).

They will come from the east and the west, from the north and the south, and sit down in the kingdom of God (*Luke 13:29*).

At the last supper Jesus held up the cup and announced He would not drink it again until He drank it new with His followers in the Kingdom (Mark 14:25). This was the last time He ate the Passover with His disciples. Believers, however, are reminded of their future meal with the Messiah in the heavenly Kingdom each time they drink the Communion cup and eat the bread.

Now when one of those who sat at the table with Him heard these things, he said to Him, "Blessed is he who shall eat bread in the kingdom of God" (*Luke 14:15*).

The Communion Meal and the *Didache*

One of the oldest manuscripts that describe some of the earliest Christian teachings is called the *Didache*. This manuscript, discovered in 1873, was translated in 1883.

Scholars fix the date of the writing at about A.D. 100 to 120. This is about the same general time frame in which the apostle John compiled Revelation, the last Book of the New Testament.

The *Didache* contains several important concepts that were taught in the first century. The first part of the manuscript describes "Two Paths of Life and Death," dealing with Christian behavior and morality in life. For example, it is written, "Do not abort a fetus or kill a child that is born."

It instructs believers to pray the Lord's Prayer three times a day. It also admonishes believers to fast twice a week—on Wednesdays and Fridays. One interesting instruction deals with baptism in water:

> Now concerning baptism, baptize as follows: after you have reviewed all these things, baptize in the name of the Father and of the Son and of the Holy Spirit in running water. But if you have no running water, then baptize in some other water; and if you are not able to baptize in cold water, then do so in warm. But if you have neither, then pour water on the head three times in the name of the Father and Son and Holy Spirit (Didache 7:1-3).

The Communion Meal is also discussed in the *Didache*:

> On the Lord's own day gather together and break bread and give thanks, having first confessed your sins so that your sacrifice may be pure. But let no one who has a quarrel with a companion join until he has been reconciled (Didache 14:1, 2).

This is the same emphasis made throughout the Scriptures. A believer should not attempt to offer a gift at the altar until he is first reconciled to his brother (Matthew 5:23, 24). Christ also taught that if a believer did not forgive his brother's trespass, he himself could not be forgiven (Matthew 6:14, 15).

According to the *Didache*, the following prayers were offered, first over the fruit of the vine and then the bread:

> We give you thanks our Father, for the holy wine of David Your servant, which You have made known to us through Jesus, Your servant; to You be the glory forever (Didache 9:2).

> We give thanks, our Father, for the life and knowledge which You have made known to us through Jesus, Your servant; to You be glory forever. Just as this broken bread was scattered upon the mountains and then was gathered

> together and became one, so may Your church
> be gathered together from the ends of the
> earth into Your kingdom; for Yours is the glory
> and the power through Jesus Christ forever
> (Didache 9:3, 4).

According to this early Christian document, a third prayer was prayed after the conclusion of the meal.

> To us You have graciously given spiritual food
> and drink, and eternal life through Your
> servant. Gather Your church from the four
> winds into your kingdom, which You have
> prepared for it: for Yours is the power and
> glory forever. May grace come, and may this
> world pass away. Hosanna to the God of
> David. If anyone is holy, let him come, if
> anyone is not, let him repent Maranatha!
> Amen (*Didache* 10:5, 9-14)!

Several points should be made here:

First, notice that David, not Abraham, is mentioned in two of three prayers. This may be because the promise of the Messiah was through the linage of David.

Abraham was promised the *land of Israel*, but David was promised the *kingdom of the world to come*. Since the Communion meal looks forward to the future Kingdom, then David, as the heir to the future kingdom, would be mentioned in the Communion prayers.

Second, in two of the three prayers there is a request to gather the church from the four winds. This theme of the gathering of the church was revealed by the apostle Paul in 1 Thessalonians 4:16, 17, and in Ephesians 1:9, 10. It is the moment when the dead in Christ will be raised and the living saints will be changed from mortal to immortal.

Together, they will be caught up to meet the Lord in the air! Paul calls the event the "gathering together unto [Christ]" in 2 Thessalonians 2:1.

At the Last Supper, Christ said He would not eat or drink again until He did so in the Kingdom. He said that when we partake of the meal, we will show forth His death until He comes. The Communion is a reminder that He will gather us together into the Kingdom!

The third interesting observation is the third prayer and the word *Maranatha*. The same word is found in 1 Corinthians 16:22, where Paul is closing his letter by saying, "If any one has no love for the Lord, let him be anathema (this means cursed or separated). Paul then says, "Maranatha!"

This is an Aramaic word meaning "our Lord comes." Because the word is an Aramaic word and not a Hebrew or Greek word, some suggest that it was invented by the early Christians as some form of a code word to identify the real believers in times of persecution.

The Three Meals of the Sabbath

Even today among the religious Jews, the Sabbath is a very important day. God established six days in which to work and the seventh day as a time of rest. A heavenly Sabbath rest is alluded to in Hebrews by Paul as our time with Christ in heaven. This will be the believers' eternal Sabbath rest (Hebrews 4:1-11).

According to Jewish mystical commentaries, there are three meals on the Sabbath day:

> Therefore one must wholeheartedly rejoice in these meals, and complete their number (three altogether), for they are meals of the perfect Faith, the Faith of the holy seed of Israel, their supernal Faith, which is not that of the heathen nations (Zohar 2:88).

The third meal was identified in early Judiasm as the "holy meal of the Ancient one" or the "meal of the King."

It was sometimes called "escorting the queen," which described the festivities that concluded the Jewish Sabbath. Jewish sages also called it the "Meal of the Messiah."

Acts 20 may be alluding to this third meal. Paul ministered in Troas for seven days, and at the conclusion of the Sabbath he preached "until midnight." As the oil lamps burned late that night, Eutychus, a young man sitting on a window ledge, fell to the ground three stories below.

The fall killed the fellow, but Paul prayed for him and the young man was raised up. Paul went back to the upper room and "broke bread and ate." He continued to speak with them until daybreak (Acts 20:7-12). After this "late night" (third meal), Paul continued his discussion. This was a normal activity after the third meal was eaten.

The third meal often pointed to the return of the Messiah and the coming Kingdom. . . .

The final discussion at the third meal often points to the return of the Messiah and the coming Kingdom. Therefore the third Sabbath meal is a special meal identifying the Meal of the Messiah.

The Lord's Table and Reconciliation

Paul refers to the Communion as the "Lord's Table" (1 Corinthians 10:21). Paul may have been comparing this with the Table of Showbread in the Temple. This golden table contained 12 pieces of holy bread, one for each of the 12 tribes of Israel.

Each week the priests were permitted to eat the 12 loaves from this table. At the same time another set of priests would bake fresh bread to replace the eaten bread, and the following week that bread was eaten and replaced.

The idea of the Table of the Lord is linked to the bread used in the Communion. Christ said He was the "bread come down from heaven," and instructed us to "eat his flesh and drink his blood" in order to have life (see John 5:30-61). This can only allude to the Communion meal, or *The Meal That Heals*!

> After the destruction of the Jewish Temple in A.D. 70, the Jews wrote in the *Talmud* that "as long as the Temple stood, the altar at the Temple atoned for Israel; but now a man's table atones for him" (Berakhoth 55, 1).

The Temple stood in Christ's time, and He and His disciples were often seen in the sacred compound. Once

Christ said that if a man were to bring a gift to the altar and there remember he had an ought against his brother, he was not to give his gift until he was reconciled to his brother (Matthew 5:23, 24).

This was the emphasis of the apostle Paul when he said we should examine ourselves when we are sitting with our brothers and sisters at the Lord's Table.

> But let a man examine himself, and so let him eat of the bread, and drink of the cup (*1 Corinthians 11:28*).

This self-examination is for the purpose of looking inwardly to examine one's relationship with God and man. Since the brass altar no longer exists in the Temple in Jerusalem, the Lord's Table becomes the "altar" of examination. Before receiving the bread and the cup, one should repent to God and then repent and make reconciliation with fellow believers.

After years of travel and ministry, I have come to believe that the three greatest spiritual hindrances to most Christians are unforgiveness, bitterness and strife. These were issues the church at Corinth dealt with. Paul told them they were filled with contentions and that many among them were weak and sickly (1 Corinthians 11:30).

Receiving Communion is not only remembering the atonement of Christ, but it is also a reminder of the coming Kingdom and the banquet of the King we will share when we enter the New Jerusalem.

> "Let us be glad and rejoice and give Him glory, for the marriage of the Lamb has come, and His wife has made herself ready." And to her it was granted to be arrayed in fine linen, clean and bright, for the fine linen is the righteous acts of the saints. Then [the voice] said to me, "Write: 'Blessed are those who are called to the marriage supper of the Lamb!'" And he said to me, "These are the true sayings of God" (*Revelation 19:7-9*).

The Climax of the Communion Meal

When the saints of all ages are caught up to meet the Lord in the air (1 Thessalonians 4:16, 17) and we enter the Kingdom of heaven, we will enjoy the final Communion meal in which covenant with our bridegroom, Jesus Christ, will consummate at the Marriage Supper of the Lamb. This Supper will be conducted at the great banquet facilities in the heavenly city, just prior to the return of Christ to set up an earthly Kingdom in Jerusalem.

Soon after the Last Supper, Jesus became the ultimate sacrificial Passover Lamb. He suffered on the cross to deliver His people from their sins. Jesus keenly desired to eat that last Passover with His disciples:

> Then He said to them, "With fervent desire I have desired to eat this Passover with you before I suffer; for I say to you, I will no longer eat of it until it is fulfilled in the kingdom of God" (*Luke 22:15, 16*).

The Last Supper and the early church's Lord's Suppers all looked forward to a fulfillment in the wedding supper of the Lamb. John wrote about the fulfillment of this Supper in Revelation 19:6-9:

> I heard . . . the voice of a great multitude, as the sound of many waters and as the sound of mighty thunderings, saying, "Alleluia! For the Lord God Omnipotent reigns! Let us be glad and rejoice and give Him glory, for the marriage of the Lamb has come, and His wife has made herself ready." And to her it was granted to be arrayed in fine linen, clean and bright, for the fine linen is the righteous acts of the saints. Then he said to me, "Write: 'Blessed are those who are called to the marriage supper of the Lamb'" (*Revelation 19:6-9*)!

This future wedding banquet weighed heavily on our Lord's mind that particular Passover evening.

> At the beginning of the feast, He said: "I will no longer eat of it until it is fulfilled in the kingdom of God" (*Luke 22:16*).

> When He passed the cup, He said: "I will not drink of the fruit of the vine until the kingdom of God comes" (*Luke 22:18*).

> After supper, He said: "I bestow upon you a kingdom . . . that you may eat and drink at My table in My kingdom" (*Luke 22:29, 30*).

Once we have entered the heavenly Kingdom, through death or through the return of Christ, there will be no pain, no sorrow, no sickness and no tears in that heavenly Kingdom. Until that time we continue to drink from the cup of redemption and eat of the bread of His presence in the Communion meal.

The cup and the bread represent His blood and His body. This meal will sustain us in body, soul and spirit until we enter the heavenly realm of perfection and glory. Then, in the Holy City, we will join together with the saints of all ages to celebrate the Banquet of the Messiah!

How to Receive the Communion Meal

When [Jesus] had given thanks, He broke [the bread] and said, "Take, eat. . . . In the same manner He also took the cup . . . saying, "This cup is the new covenant in My blood *(1 Corinthians 11:24, 25).*

$\mathfrak{T}$he Lord's Supper not only shows forth the Lord's death until He comes, but it helps to keep a believer in right relationship with God and with his fellow man. As previously emphasized, this is accomplished through the procedure of self-examination, prior to receiving the

Supper. I have outlined four steps a believer should take when receiving the Communion meal:

Look Inward

Prior to receiving Communion, a believer should look inward into their heart and spirit. This inward examination is to ensure that you have no hidden or known sin in your life. The Bible says, "But let a man examine himself" (1 Corinthians 11:28).

The word *examine* means "to reach a result from an inquiry." Ask yourself if you have offended God in word or deed. Is there a bondage or a pet sin that you are struggling with? If the answer is yes, you should repent before receiving Communion. This action will help keep your spirit pure between you and God.

Look Outward

Prior to receiving Communion, we must look outward toward those we know, including family, friends, or fellow believers. The Bible teaches that, if we have something against a fellow believer, our gift (offerings) will not be blessed until we first go to our brother or sister in Christ and make restitution (amends) with the person:

> Therefore if you bring your gift to the altar, and there remember that your brother has something against you, leave your gift there before the altar, and go your way. First be reconciled to your brother, and then come and offer your gift *(Matthew 5:23, 24)*.

Restitution, or reconciliation, is the theme of the New Covenant. If Christ forgave us, then we should forgive others. Your faith in the Cross and the suffering of Christ has built a bridge between you and God . . . and between earth and eternity!

Your relationship with God is vertical and your relationship with man is horizontal. When a vertical and a horizontal line intersect, they form a cross.

Look Upward

Believers who eat the bread and drink the cup should meditate on Christ's redemptive work. They should remember that He suffered on our behalf. Through His sacrificial death and triumphant resurrection, we can enjoy a threefold atonement. We can be made whole in spirits, souls and bodies. Looking upward to our High Priest, Jesus Christ, we should meditate on the goodness of God and on His mercy toward us.

Look Onward

Live every day with the expectancy that you will fulfill your God-given assignments and will live out all of your days. Seize the promise of Psalms 91:16: "With long life I will satisfy him, and show him My salvation."

One of the great faith ministers of yesteryear was Smith Wigglesworth. In his earlier days, Smith was healed and he emphasized the healing gifts throughout his long ministry. Even in those days, he received the revelation of daily Communion.

Wigglesworth lived to be 87 years of age, and passed away quietly while in a church service. This is the way to go—live out your assigned days and go to sleep in Christ!

The Communion Procedure

The actual unleavened bread used at a Jewish Passover is called *matzo bread*. It is available at certain grocery stores; but if it is not available in your area, you may use unsalted crackers. When this is not available, use simple bread. The Lord knows your heart and the effort you are making to obey Him. For the fruit of the vine, I personally use grape juice obtained from a local grocery store.

In fact, a certain brand of grape juice was first developed *for* Communion. Dr. Thomas B. Welch was born in England in 1825 and became a dentist. He was a Methodist minister for a few years before he took up the practice of dentistry in Vineland, New Jersey. Dr. Welch did not like to see intoxicating wine being used in his own church's Communion service.

In 1869, he developed a process that kept grape juice from fermenting. He called the product "Dr. Welch's Unfermented Wine," and tried to persuade churches

Dr. Welch developed a process that kept grape juice from formenting, calling the product "Unfermented Wine."

to use it in Communion. He met with great resistance from the churches, however.

For 20 years Dr. Welch's Unfermented Wine was a family refreshment in the Welch household, but he could persuade only a few churches to use it for Communion. Welch's youngest son, Charles, became convinced, however, that it had commercial potential. He was also a dentist in Vineland.

Charles borrowed $5,000 from his father and set up a juice production facility on the family's property. To make the product more commercially appealing, he changed its name to Welch's Grape Juice.

The following year, Charles introduced his beverage at the Columbian Exposition in Chicago, and gave out free samples of Welch's Grape Juice to millions of fair-goers. The rest, as they say, is history. The product remains unchanged to this day.

Some people purchase an actual Passover (Seder) cup for Communion. Any type of cup may be used at home; and you may, as I do, want to set aside a cup just for this purpose. (Our ministry has a portable Communion kit you may order).

If you are receiving Communion the first thing in the morning, clear your mind and heart of all distractions and fully concentrate on the wonderful grace of God. Pour the fruit of the vine into the cup, take a piece of bread in your hand and, praying in your own words, bless the bread and the cup. Thank God for sending Christ to redeem you.

If you are in need of healing, begin to quote the promise: "With the stripes of Jesus I am healed" (see Isaiah

53:5; 1 Peter 2:24). In prayer, tell the Lord you believe that the blood of Christ was shed for your atonement, including your physical healing. Believe, as you receive the Communion, that the life of Christ is working in your body, driving out every sickness, disease, and weakness that is hindering your life.

Remember that this is not a magical formula. Instead, it is a sacred moment between you and your heavenly Father. If a person does not receive Communion every day, I recommend that they do so at least once a week. Do not allow this act to become a religious ritual where you lose the meaning.

Prayer Prior to Receiving Communion

Here is a sample prayer that you may pray. As you grow in the grace and knowledge of God, you will learn to pray a simple prayer from your heart.

Heavenly Father, I thank You for sending Your Son, Jesus Christ, to redeem mankind. I thank You that through His sufferings, Christ purchased a threefold redemption for my spirit, mind and body. Today, I ask you to bless this bread that represents the body of Christ. Bless the fruit of the vine that represents the precious blood of Christ.

Father, as you have forgiven me, so I forgive those who have sinned against me. Lord, I forgive and release anyone who has wronged me, and I ask You to search my spirit and remove any trace of sin or disobedience from my life. Today, I release from my mental prison anyone who has hurt me in any way, and I ask You to bless them and help them spiritually.

Father, as I receive this Communion, I ask You to bring strength and health to me spiritually, emotionally, and physically, because of the New Covenant that was sealed through the sufferings of Christ. Father, Jesus carried my infirmities; therefore, I ask You to lift from me what Jesus has carried for Me. I receive it by faith, and I give You all the glory and honor, in the name of Jesus Christ. Amen.

Spend time praying, meditating, and praising the Lord for your salvation, your healing and your wholeness. Remember that this is a reminder of the covenant, and God is moved by His covenant!

Concluding Thoughts

After many years of full time ministry, I have discovered an important key connected to receiving from the Lord. All truth must be processed through the intellect, where we reason and weigh the evidence we receive:

> "Come now, and let us reason together," says the Lord *(Isaiah 1:18)*.

Yet, for spiritual truth to impact your life, it must be quickened to your inner spirit. As the psalmist once said:

> Remember the word unto thy servant, upon which thou hast caused me to hope. This is my comfort in my affliction: for thy word hath quickened me *(Psalms 119:49, 50)*.

The word *quickened* means "to make alive." There are times when you hear a message from God's Word and you are intellectually challenged. At other times, you are simply uplifted and blessed. There are occasions when the Word of God pierces your soul like a sword (Hebrews 4:12).

Then there are unique times when the message you are hearing or the book you are reading seems to come alive in your spirit. You know when this happens. The information becomes revelation as the eyes of your understanding are opened (see Ephesians 1:18). The truth seems to jump from the pages, and suddenly you can sense a strong witness inwardly that God will move on your behalf.

The spiritual truth you read must become more than a book in your hands for it to be a message that will impact your life. The Word of God must quicken your heart and spirit.

When the written or spoken Word of God becomes alive and energized in your heart, it becomes a *rhema* word. The word *rhema* is one of the Greek words translated in the New Testament as "Word of God."

When the written or spoken Word of God comes alive in your heart and energizes you, it becomes a "rhema" word. . . .

Two examples where the word *rhema* is translated as Word of God are:

> So then faith comes by hearing, and hearing by the word (*rhema*) of God *(Romans 10:17).*

> And take the helmet of salvation, and the sword of the Spirit, which is the word (*rhema*) of God *(Ephesians 6:17).*

Once the Word of God moves from intellectual reasoning to a quickened, living word in your spirit, then faith will enter your spirit! You are able to believe what God has spoken and respond to His Word in faith.

This has personally happened to me on several occasions. I recall praying for several months for direction in my ministry. During a special service in Ohio, the Holy Spirit quickened my spirit to act on my faith, and as I obeyed, the Lord would meet the needs of our ministry. I acted in faith, and He met the needs.

I want to emphasize again that the concept of Communion is Biblical and should be practiced, whether or not a person is physically sick. If you attend a church where Communion is offered, then by all means receive the blessed Sacrament. Examine your relationship with God and with man, and repent to both, if necessary.

In Judaism, a distinction is made between sins against God and sins against a fellow man. This is clear from the Old Testament sacrifices. One offering known as a sin offering, was a sacrifice made when one sinned against the Word of God.

The other offering, known as a guilt offering, was made as a form of restitution when a person sinned against a fellow man. The guilty person not only went before God for forgiveness, but also before the person against whom he had sinned. This is why Jesus said:

> Therefore if you bring your gift to the altar, and there remember that your brother has something against you, leave your gift there before the altar, and go your way. First be reconciled to your brother, and then come and offer your gift *(Matthew 5:23, 24).*

Just as Jesus would say "Again I say unto you" (Matthew 19:24), I wish to remind you that one of the greatest roadblocks to healing is unforgiveness and strife. You will never receive your complete healing if you continually allow strife and contention to rule your life. Both my father and I have seen people receive wonderful answers to prayer after they began confessing their faults and forgiving those who have mistreated them (James 5:16).

In conclusion, I am emphasizing inner cleansing through repentance, because I do not want to see this powerful Covenant of Healing through the Lord's Supper become null and void due to a hidden sin or attitude that is unconfessed and forsaken.

I emphasize again that this is not magic, nor is it medicine. Each person must judge this teaching in his or her own spirit, and act accordingly. Whether we receive Communion daily, weekly or monthly, we must do it in a spirit of understanding and faith.

I believe it is Biblical for us to live out our appointed days and then depart in peace. *The Meal That Heals* gives you the Biblical revelation that God has established to help you do just that.

15 Most-Asked Questions about Daily Communion

Question 1: *If someone is persuaded to receive Communion, but does not believe it has the power to bring healing, will the healing power still work—even though the person does not believe?*

Answer: Some Christians understand only the salvation part of the atonement. They do not believe in any form of healing, especially physical healing. All blessings in the New Covenant operate through faith. Salvation is received by faith. Deliverance is received by faith. So is the Holy Spirit Baptism.

Since all the blessings of the New Covenant are activated by faith, healing is also received by faith. No aspect of the covenant will work if a person does not have faith. The Bible says:

> For indeed the gospel was preached to us as well as to them; but the word which they heard did not profit them, not being mixed with faith in those who heard it. For we who have believed do enter that rest (*Hebrews 4:2, 3*).

Question 2: *My pastor told me that only an ordained minister is permitted to perform the Lord's Supper. He said the teaching of daily communion was not Biblical.*

Answer: As you have seen in this book, we have proven from Scripture and history that the Communion teaching is thoroughly Biblical for sincere believers. The practice of daily Communion was common in the first century, although it was later lost through man-made traditions.

In a local church assembly the minister (pastor or priest) overseeing the assembly should perform the service. When this practice is observed from house to house, however, individual believers are "kings and priests unto God" and may administer Communion (Revelation 1:6).

Question 3: *I helped my husband receive Communion for several weeks before he passed away. I began feeling*

*that it really doesn't work, or my husband would have been
healed. Can you help me with this?*

Answer: I do not know the circumstances of the situation with your husband, so I cannot address your particular issue directly. It is as important, however, for the person receiving Communion to have faith as it is for the one giving the Communion Supper.

"Will . . . unbelief make the faithfulness of God without effect? Certainly not" (Romans 3:3, 4)!

We all have to remember that it is appointed unto men once to die (Hebrews 9:27). If we receive Communion every day, and live to be 100, eventually we will die. Communion cannot keep a person alive forever.

The second point I want to make is that a person can enter the kingdom of heaven, even if he dies from sickness. The Bible says of a great prophet: "Elisha had become sick with the illness of which he would die" (2 Kings 13:14). If a person does all he can to be healed, and passes away, we must trust the Lord that He knows what is best and has deeper plans, of which we are not aware.

One must not miss the true, personal meaning of the Communion—to bring the believer into a more personal and intimate relationship with Christ.

Question 4: *Should a person use fermented wine or simple grape juice when receiving the Communion?*

Answer: When Jesus held up the cup and introduced the New Covenant he called the cup the "fruit of the vine" (Matthew 26:29; Mark 14:25; Luke 22:18). According to historical sources, when wine was used at the Passover, a cup was mixed with three parts water and one part wine. This ensured believers that no alcohol would be active.

Jesus Christ was sinless. In the Bible, normal bread contained leaven. Wine which sits for a long time becomes fermented.

In Scripture, leaven represents sin. The bread at Passover and at Communion had no leaven, because Christ was without sin. Fermentation in wine occurs when the juice begins to break down and, with the help of bacteria, sugar turns into alcohol. Fermented wine has gone through this decaying process.

Because the fruit of the vine is a picture of the blood of Christ, and Christ's blood was pure and untainted by the sin nature of Adam, I believe it is preferable to use pure grape juice.

Question 5: *What type of bread should be used during Communion?*

Answer: Often, a local church will use a small round wafer that is available through Christian book stores. Others use a small cracker. I personally prefer to use the Jewish matzo bread, which is a perfect picture of the body of our Lord. This bread is usually available in most major grocery stores.

When a person cannot or does not have access to this type of bread, then regular bread may be used. God understands each situation, and the faith of God's obedient servants is what is important.

Question 6: *I am a prisoner. I cannot get grape juice for Communion, and it is impossible for me to get the Jewish bread. I want to receive Communion, however. Will the Lord still honor my faith, even though I am unable to obtain the juice and the bread?*

Answer: I am reminded of the commentary on water baptism in the Didache, which is from the first century.

> But concerning baptism, thus baptize ye: having first recited all these precepts, baptize in the name of the Father, and of the Son, and of the Holy Spirit, in running water; but if thou hast not running water, baptize in some other water, and if thou canst not baptize in cold, in warm water; but if thou hast neither, pour water three times

on the head, in the name of the Father, and of the Son, and of the Holy Spirit (*Didache 7:1-3*).

I believe God honors the sincere heart, and understands the situation you are in. I suggest you use whatever you can. Ask the Lord to bless it as you enjoy Communion with Him.

Question 7: *Don't you believe that if a person receives Communion too often it will become commonplace and soon lose its effectiveness?*

Answer: This is like saying if I read the Bible too often I will tire of the Scriptures. Or if I pray too much I may lose sight of prayer. A person who loves Christ will never fear that spending too much time with Him, including the Communion, will water down the awe and majesty of intimacy with Him.Regular Communion does not cause one to become indifferent when he understands the power of intimacy with Christ through the bread and the cup.

Question 8: *Among the early church fathers the Communion is called the* Eucharist. *What is the meaning of this word and why is it not used today?*

Answer: Most Christians observe the Communion as a binding obligation. In church it is variously referred to as the **Lord's Supper, Holy Communion** or the **Eucharist.**

The word *eucharist* is from the Greek and means "thanksgiving." The noun and its verb form (to give thanks) are found in 55 verses of the New Testament. Four tell of Jesus giving thanks before He declared the bread and the cup to be His body and His blood (Matthew 26:27, Mark 14:23, Luke 22:19, 1 Corinthians 11:24).

Our Catholic friends call this observance the *Eucharist* because, they say, when the priest blesses the elements, they become the sacrifice for our sins and our healing. Often, the term is used synonymously with "Mass."

While some Protestants use the term *Eucharist*, most prefer **Communion** or the **Lord's Supper**. The Bible calls it **Communion** in 1 Corinthians 10:16:

The cup of blessing which we bless, is it not the communion of the blood of Christ? The bread which we break, is it not the communion of the body of Christ (1 Corinthians 10:16)?

Notice that Paul called the cup, "the cup of blessing." He called Communion **"the Lord's table"** in verse 21.

Despite various interpretations and different ways to refer to this important rite, Christ's commandment, "Do this in remembrance of Me," has been obeyed by Christians through the centuries.

The Bible does not require us to use any certain term, and it doesn't forbid us to use any particular term. Call it either or both, but I prefer to call it *The Meal That Heals*! When we participate:

- ✝ It reminds Jesus of the New Covenant He has made with us.
- ✝ It brings us into a relationship of closer unity with God.
- ✝ It fosters an intimate communion with our Lord and Savior.
- ✝ It points to the coming wedding banquet in heaven.

Question 9: *I was raised Catholic and in the church we were taught that the host (wafer) becomes the literal body of Christ and the wine becomes the literal blood of Christ. Why do many ministers teach that the bread and wine represent the body of Christ, and it does not become the body of Christ?*

Answer: Catholic doctrine says that at Mass the bread and wine become the body and blood of Christ the moment the priest blesses the host. This is called *transubstantiation*. It cannot be true for the following reasons:

- ✝ Christ, in His resurrected and glorified body, ascended to heaven and is now at the right hand of God (Acts 1:9; 7:55, 56; Romans 8:34; Colossians 3:1; Hebrews 10:12; 12:2; 1 Peter 3:22).

✟ Although Christ's presence is everywhere, His physical body is one, and is not divided. He does not have thousands of bodies all over the world that can be broken at every Communion. In Communion, we break the bread, not the body of Christ.

Question 10: *What is the difference between a Catholic Mass and a Protestant Communion Service?*

Answer: There are many theological and cultural differences, but because that is not the emphasis in this book, I will list only a few:

✟ Catholic Mass is called "a sacrifice" for the forgiveness of sins; Protestant Communion is a memorial, a communion, a feast of thanksgiving; not a sacrifice for sin.

✟ Catholic Mass claims to repeat the atoning sacrifice of Christ on Calvary; Protestant Communion obeys Christ's command to observe this meal until He returns.

✟ Catholic Mass claims to change the elements into the actual body and blood of the Lord Jesus Christ; Protestant Communion sees the elements as symbols of His body and blood.

✟ Catholic Mass says you offer the body of Jesus for your sins each time you observe the Mass; Protestants believe the body of Christ was offered by the Lord himself "once for all" (Hebrews 10:10).

✝ In Catholic Mass, the priest "breaks off a small piece of the Body of Christ" in preparation for "serving the host"; in Protestant Communion, the minister breaks the bread, not the body of Christ.

✝ In Catholic Mass, the elements are "mingled" by the priest; in Protestant Communion, the elements are given and received separately, as indicated in Scripture.

Question 11: *How old should a person be before he or she is permitted to receive the Communion?*

Answer: This is like asking, "How old should a person be before he or she receives Christ as Savior? Or, "How old should a person be before he or she is baptized in water?" Although a small child is innocent of practicing sin, the child should be taught the plan of salvation once he or she can understand the concept of redemption and can pray a prayer to receive Christ.

If one can understand God's plan of salvation, he can also understand the importance of water baptism. Once a child grasps the meaning and importance of these concepts, I believe it is in order for the child to receive the Communion.

No place in the Bible indicates the age of a person receiving Communion, although the *Didache* taught that a person should be baptized in water before receiving.

Question 12: *If a person is living a life of hidden sin, should that person receive Communion? Is this receiving it unworthily?*

Answer: When Ananias and Sapphira lied to the Holy Spirit, they were both struck dead (Acts 5:3). After Simon the Sorcerer was baptized in water, he continued his occult practice and Peter rebuked him, telling him he was going to perish if he didn't repent (Acts 8:18-24).

Sin among so-called believers is very serious because a believer knows better. They are sinning with knowledge!

When my dad was a pastor, some people would not come to church to receive Communion because they said, "We have some things in our life and don't feel worthy." Actually, they judged their own spiritual condition by this statement! If they weren't prepared for Communion, they wouldn't be prepared for Christ's coming!

A Christian should use the occasion of Communion to judge themselves and to repent to God and make reconciliation with fellow believers before receiving. Otherwise they could "eat and drink condemnation to themselves" (1 Corinthians 11:29).

Question 13: *When do you personally receive Communion? Is there a set time of the day, week or month?*

Answer: I especially receive Communion when I am sensing a spiritual warfare . . . or when I feel I need more intimate time with God . . . or if I am encountering a physical attack against my body.

I often have one of my workers in the office to prepare the bread and juice, and then we pray together as I receive the Communion.

I also receive it at my home church where the family attends. I suggest to those who are suffereing from a sickness or disease, however, to receive the Communion every day if possible.

Question 14: *If I am sick and am believing the Lord to heal my body, will it happen instantly or gradually? How will I know I am healed?*

Answer: It can happen instantly or gradually. Do not quit taking medication from a doctor, unless the physician tells you that you are now free from the illness, or you no longer need the medication. Most people will know when the healing has occurred by the symptoms stopping or by a medical checkup.

Question 15: *My family thinks that receiving Communion at home is some type of a new religious cult. They are very traditional. How can I convince them otherwise?*

Answer: Ask them to read this book and be open to the Word of God, and I believe they will understand the concept. If not, then hide the revelation in your own heart and do not argue with them or try to convince them. It will only cause your own heart to grieve more. Agree where you can agree and stay at peace where you can stay at peace.

My Final Word to You

After ministering several years on the subject of daily Communion, I have been amazed and blessed to hear so many testimonies of men and women of all denominational backgrounds who received this renewed truth in their hearts and acted in faith.

Many have begun receiving the Communion on a daily basis in their homes, among family or close Christian friends. Perhaps the most remarkable testimonies have come from individuals who were diagnosed with incurable diseases or physical infirmities, and received healing through the Communion Supper.

As I have stated many times, Communion cannot keep a person alive forever in this world. Sooner or later we will die. Some depart by accidents, some through the hands of criminals and others by sickness or disease.

I am suggesting that we should not die before our appointed time. We should seek God to help us live out all of our days, so we may fulfill His assignment and destiny on our lives.

The fact is, strong Christians who pray, read the Bible, attend church, support ministries and receive Communion are happier and know better how to release stress than those who see no importance in these activities.

Bibliography

Albert Barnes, *Barnes Notes on the New Testament.*

The Catholic Encyclopedia, Volume V on CD-Rom, © 1909.

Adam Clarke, *Adam Clarke's Commentary on the Bible.*

F.C. Cook, *The Bible* Commentary, n.d.

Irenaeus, *Adversus Haereses, Book II.*

Justin Martyr, *Apologetics II*, Chapter 6.

Origen, *Contra Celsum, Book III, 24.*

Pliny, *Letters 10.96, 97*. William Whiston, tr.

Philip Schaff, *New Schaff-Herzog Encyclopedia of Religious Knowledge, Volume 7*. (New York: Funk & Wagnalls, 1908). pp. 24-40.

Thomas Whitelaw, *Preacher's Complete Homiletic Commentary on the Acts of the Apostles*. (Grand Rapids: Baker Book House, 1978). p. 475.

<http://eword.gospelcom.net/comments/acts/jfb/acts2.htm>

<http://bible.crosswalk.com/Commentaries/JamiesonFaussettBrown/jfb.cki?book=ac&chapter=002>